HORRIBLE SCIENCE

THE TERRIBLE TRUTH ABOUT TIME

NICK ARNOLD

Illustrated by
Tony De Saulles

Blue
Ribond

Scholastic Children's Books,
Commonwealth House, 1-19 New Oxford Street,
London WC1A 1NU, UK

A division of Scholastic Ltd
London ~ New York ~ Toronto ~ Sydney ~ Auckland
Mexico City ~ New Delhi ~ Hong Kong

First published in the UK by Scholastic Ltd, 2002

Text copyright © Nick Arnold, 2002
Illustrations copyright © Tony De Saulles, 2002

ISBN 0 439 98227 8

Typeset by Falcon Oast Graphic Art, East Hoathly, Sussex.
Printed and bound in Great Britain by Cox & Wyman Ltd, Reading, Berkshire.

2 4 6 8 10 9 7 5 3 1

The right of Nick Arnold and Tony De Saulles to be identified as the author and
illustrator of this work respectively has been asserted by them in accordance
with the Copyright, Designs and Patents Act, 1988.

Contents

THANKS!

WELL, THERE'S NO PRESENT LIKE THE TIME!

Nick Arnold has been writing stories and books since he was a youngster, but never dreamt he'd find fame writing about time. His research involved timing snails and being kidnapped by aliens and he enjoyed every minute of it.

When he's not delving into Horrible Science, he spends his spare time eating pizza, riding his bike and thinking up corny jokes (though not all at the same time).

Tony De Saulles picked up his crayons when he was still in nappies and has been doodling ever since. He takes Horrible Science very seriously and even agreed to test a time machine. Fortunately, he has made a full recovery.

When he's not out with his sketchpad, Tony likes to write poetry and play squash, though he hasn't written any poetry about squash yet.

INTRODUCTION

Everyone knows about time. We have spare time, we gain time, we lose time. We mark time, keep time, play for time, but in the end time waits for no one. You can tell the time from a clock, but few people can handle the really tricky time questions.

HOW OLD ARE THE STARS?

THEY'RE AS OLD AS TIME.

SO HOW OLD'S THAT?

ER...

WHAT WAS THERE BEFORE TIME?

ER — ASK YOUR MUM.

WHAT IS TIME?

TIME TO GO TO BED!

See what I mean...?!

So, where do you look for the truth about time? Well, you could ask an expert. But you might need a brain as big as an elephant to understand their answers…

But there is another way … you could read this book! It tells the greatest mystery story ever: the story of how some people tried to find the truth about time by measuring it and experimenting with it, and others have even dreamt of travelling through it…

Any good book will carry you away to other times and distant places. But this book takes you far, far further on a trek through time and space to seek out some of the strangest science ever. You'll also meet some seriously suffering scientists. But hold on – I mustn't tell you everything now! You'd best read on and find out the Terrible Truth for yourself…

IT'S ABOUT TIME

Here's a terribly tricky thought:

TIME IS LIKE AN ONION...

No, I don't mean that the topic of time has a bitter taste and gives you bad breath and makes you cry! I mean, like an onion, time has layers; layers of knowledge and mystery. And you'll be pleased to know that we'll be exploring all these layers and uncovering some fascinating facts like...

- How it's possible to be late for everything and get away with it.
- What happens if you fall into a black hole.
- The TERRIBLE TRUTH mentioned in the title.

But let's start outside our onion (it's better than starting in the middle!). You probably learnt about time when you were little, and no wonder! Time affects us all – we measure our lives by time, we plan our days by time, and we're always running out of time. Especially on a Sunday evening when the weekend's almost over and the dog needs to go walkies.

But now for a question that makes scientists froth at the mouth. You see, the answer's *terribly* complicated...

OK, OK – I'll try to answer it myself…

Terrible time fact file

NAME: Time

THE BASIC FACTS: 1 Time is the on-going existence of the universe. Right now you're experiencing the moment in time known as "now" or "the present". With me so far?

THIS IS THE PRESENT!

I CAN'T SEE ANY PRESENTS

BEGINNING OF TIME

BIG BANG!

2 Time began with "the big bang". That's when the universe kicked off as an unimaginably tiny point in space. No one knows where the universe came from, but it's been getting bigger ever since.

3 Scientists believe that space and time are part of the same thing. But if that sounds a bit brain-boggling – don't panic! You don't need to get your head round it until page 107.

FROTH! PANIC!

NOW YOU KNOW HOW THE SCIENTIST ON PAGE 7 FEELS

8

TERRIBLE DETAILS: Many of life's misfortunes can be put down to being in the wrong place at the wrong time. Ever missed a train, a plane, a bus or a boat? Ever turned up for a fancy dress party on the wrong day? You'll know *exactly* what I mean!

IT'S TOMORROW BUT YOU CAN WAIT IN THE LIVING ROOM.

Bet you never knew!
1 The smallest amount of time that can possibly be measured is 0.00000000000000000000000000000 00000000000001 of a second – that's six hundred million billion billion billion billionths of a minute. This teeny-weeny fragment of time is called "Planck time". It's not to be confused with...

a) A plank of wood.

b) Walking the plank – that's how pirates were said to get rid of their victims.

c) Being as thick as a plank.

It's actually named after German scientist Max Planck (1858–1947) who made the calculation. Mind you, although Planck time is less than the blink of a gnat's eyelid, it's probably twice as long as it takes most children to open their Christmas presents. 2 The largest amount of time is the existence of the universe – roughly 13 billion years. That is a very long time – I mean, in that time 185 million people might have lived one after the other. That's if people had been around at the start of the universe!

So people have had stacks of time to wonder what time is and how it all began. Unfortunately, without this book to help them, they had to come up with their own ideas.

There are stories about time from all over the world – here's one from ancient Greece…

A terribly sick-ly story

The god of time was called Kronos*. He was the son of the god of the sky and the goddess of the Earth.

*Kronos means "time" in Ancient Greek.

One day Kronos had a big row with his dad. He took a sickle, that's a tool with a curved blade, and chopped his dad into bits.

I'VE TAUGHT HIM A SHARP LESSON.

Then Kronos married his own sister...

WHAT, MARRY ME UGLY SISTER? YOU'RE JOKIN'!

THERE'S NOT MUCH CHOICE, BRUV, 'COS I'M THE ONLY GIRL IN THE WORLD!

Kronos reckoned that one day his children would steal his power – so he swallowed his kids.

I LOVE BABY FOOD

After Kronos had gulped down a few little baby gods and goddesses, Mrs K hatched a plan. She wrapped a big boulder up like a baby and gave it to her hungry hubbie.

OH, THAT'S A BIG ONE!

But Kronos was nothing if not greedy, so he swallowed the stone without a second thought.

BURP!

Meanwhile, Mrs Kronos hid the real baby, a boy named Zeus, until he was old enough to teach his dad a few table manners.

Zeus made Kronos sick up his brothers and sisters.

SPEW!

Isn't that a pleasant little bedtime tale? To this day the old year is often pictured as an old man (known as Father Time) with a sickle, and the new year as a baby – and these characters were once Kronos and Zeus. Careful with that sickle now!

Today we know that these stories were as sensible as trying to teach opera to a tom cat – but they do show how people tried to make sense of time. Scientists, of course, have taken a more scientific approach – and we will too, in the next chapter. But you'd better hurry – the next chapter is starting now!

TERRIBLY MESSED-UP TIME

The really odd thing is that you can't see time passing – but you can see things happening as time passes. Every day the sun appears to move across the sky as the Earth spins in space, and the moon moves across the sky at night for the same reason. The seasons change more slowly. And even more gradually, people grow older.

≡NOW≡ 20 YEARS' TIME 200 YEARS' TIME

We're used to all this – aren't we? I mean, you'd be utterly stunned if things happened the opposite way round and people magically grew younger. Mind you, I bet anyone over 40 reading this would be thrilled if their wrinkles disappeared and their grey hairs faded without the aid of special shampoo!

Dare you discover ... how to see things happening backwards?

What you need:
This book
Yourself

13

What you do:

1 See this tasteful drawing of a man with his head cut off? All you do is lay the book down on a table in good light and lower your face slowly towards the chopping block. Don't panic – it's not dangerous!

2 Look at the bloody drops but don't focus on them.

You should notice:

By the time your nose is touching the page the head will be joining with the body! As your eye gets closer to the page, your field of vision narrows until you can't see the gap between the head and the body. But it looks like time is running backwards!

If you rewind a video you'll see similar effects such as explosions that make people jump to their feet. And if you watch the entire movie backwards, you'll know the end before you find out how it began. It would be a bit like travelling back in time.

Anyway, talking about time travel, it's time for the first instalment of our exclusive time-travel story…

Private eye, MI Gutzache will do anything as long as it's for money, and he's about to test a time machine for odd-ball inventor, Professor N Large. But the test goes wrong … can you spot the problem?

M.I. GUTZACHE IS LOST IN TIME

Gutzache's report

So what's a New York private eye like me doing helping out in some kind of half-ass experiment? I wish I knew. The reasons go back in time and I haven't the time to go into them. I'd done some jobs for the Prof in the past and wished I hadn't. But the pay was good and the dollars did the talking.

So there I was in the Prof's sinister science lab. I was strapped into his lousy invention like salami in a sandwich. He said it was a time machine – I guess that made me the time-machine guinea pig.

The Prof threw a switch and next thing I knew I was tucked up in bed in the Prof's spare room. I had a hunch something was wrong – but I just didn't know how wrong. I couldn't put my finger on it – but I found out soon enough.

I backed out of bed. A few jigsaw pieces fell into place – I'd lost control of my body! It had a mind of its own and that mind wasn't mine. My body wanted to move backwards – so I humoured it. At least it knew where it was going – and that was more than I did…

The next bit is kind of personal and dirty, but the Prof said "spill the beans" and I do as I'm paid. I backwards shuffled into the bathroom. I grabbed my toothbrush and turned the taps but the water flowed up from the drain. Big globs of frothy spit-like slime flew into my mouth with wet splutt sounds.

I was kind of shocked. I tried to brush my teeth – but my mouth felt foul.

"Hey, Gutzache," I thought shakily. "Get a grip, buddy!"

Feeling kind of confused, I wiped my face and hands on the towel and tried to wash. The towel made me wet and more scummy water rose from the drain and leapt into the taps. I figured the Prof could use a good plumber!

I tugged the toilet chain and then opened the lid. The pan had been used and I didn't like what I saw – but I dropped my pants and sat down. Then the contents of the bowl rose up and got sucked into my body! It was the worst moment of my life, but worse was to come…

The paper was dry as I pushed it on to the roll. I stood up. The water looked clean – but I felt dirty. The case had gotten to my nerves.

"Hey, Gutzache," I thought, "you're a detective, you've gotta figure it out!"

To cut a long story slightly less long, I changed into my clothes and somehow got downstairs – all backwards, of course. I was scared I'd fall but my body knew the steps. I could hear the Prof's voice. He wasn't talking no English I'd ever heard.

I figured it was Ancient Icelandic.

The Professor insisted on talking in this language all the time and the real weird thing was, I was talking back to him in the same tongue. I hadn't a clue what we were saying, but whatever it was it sure made sense to the Prof.

Then I found myself seated at the table for some kind of meal. And it was soon after this that I cracked the case. It was the cat that blew the cover on the entire operation.

The Prof had been bumbling around picking bits of china out of the trash and arranging them on the floor. He was muttering some clap-trap – something like: "YRROS OS M'I RAED HO!"

For some dumb reason the Professor picked up the cat and put her on the table. Then a real weird thing happened. The bits of china flew together on the floor and rose in the air like a freaky flying saucer landing right in front of me. It hit the cat's foot. And the cat took off backwards like some kind of kitty helicopter and touched down on the floor!

I've seen a few wacko things but I ain't seen nothing like that. And then I figured that I had. Last night the kitty jumped on the table and knocked my mug on the floor. Then I knew the worst. I was re-living yesterday! Time was going backwards!

I felt kind of bloated. I could feel half-chewed food rising up in my gullet and into my mouth and my spoon scooping it out of my mouth and OH HELL – it had to be the snails I ate last night! They looked just as bad second time around. In fact they looked almost as bad as I felt. I was giving up  food from my stomach and putting it back on my plate!

I was eating … backwards!

And so the day went backwards. I made a backwards flight in a backwards-flying plane. I recalled the moment when the greasy airline dinner and air turbulence made me barf. I  was praying it wouldn't happen and it did – *backwards!*

It was as bad as last time and worse. I grabbed the sick bag and the puke kinda leapt out at me. I got to catch it in my mouth and gulp it down my throat. I ended up at home in bed. It was morning. I was sleepy. It had been the worst day of my life – the wrong way round! And that's when I woke up back in the time machine…

The Professor writes…

I fixed the fault and I apologized to Mr Gutzache on behalf of myself and my cat, Tiddles. It seems Mr Gutzache experienced time running backwards although his brain was working normally. Mr Gutzache didn't feel much like his supper that evening - and, oh dear, I thought he liked snails!

Oh no, looks like the story has upset our scientific adviser for this book, self-taught time expert, Norbert Nerdworthy. I should explain that Norbert spends most of his time in his bedroom researching time science – and he's most particular about details…

Three hours later…

I really must complain about this story in the strongest possible terms!

It's quite impossible for time to run backwards! You see, it's all due to…

…and stories of this nature may give young persons of a youthful age the idea that scientific activity is fun and exciting. And we don't want to encourage that sort of thing!

Hmm – Norbert's got a point! Many scientists believe that time can't go backwards because of a very important scientific rule. This rule only works in one direction – forwards into the future. It's to do with the increase of muddle…

Terrible expressions

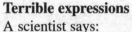

A scientist says:

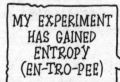

MY EXPERIMENT HAS GAINED ENTROPY (EN-TRO-PEE)

Do you say…?

GAINED A TROPHY? WELL DONE!

Scientists reckon that the amount of entropy in the universe grows over *time*. Mind you, you can get the basic idea by looking in your very own home! Do your socks vanish without trace? Do you find someone else's knickers or underpants in your drawers on a Monday morning? If so, you'll know what I mean about muddle increasing over time! But *why* does this happen? Could it be a plot by sinister scientists to make us lose our underwear? Er, no.

Terrible time fact file

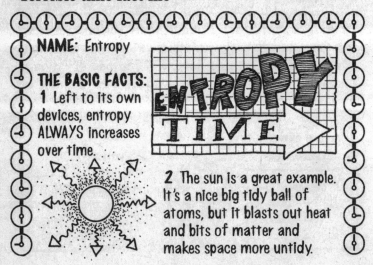

NAME: Entropy

THE BASIC FACTS:
1 Left to its own devices, entropy ALWAYS increases over time.

2 The sun is a great example. It's a nice big tidy ball of atoms, but it blasts out heat and bits of matter and makes space more untidy.

20

3 Entropy also increases over time in this lovely mug of hot chocolate topped with ice cream...

HEAT! HEAT!

HEAT ENERGY FLOWS INTO THE ICE CREAM

THE HOT CHOCOLATE HAS LOTS OF HEAT ENERGY

X-RAY VIEW OF MUG

Half an hour later...

H E A T!

THE ICE CREAM HAS MELTED. HEAT HAS ESCAPED INTO THE AIR

THE ICE CREAM IS MUDDLED WITH THE DRINK

4 And because entropy increases over time, you can actually tell the direction of time from it! Gutzache figured that time was running backwards when the mug put itself together.

In real life this doesn't happen because it would mean entropy getting less on its own. And that's why your room doesn't tidy itself — so you'd better do it *yourself*.

Of course, the discovery of entropy and the direction of time was a giant leap forward for science. You'd probably like to think that the scientist who explained what was happening would become rich and famous and live happily ever after. Well, science ain't that nice...

Hall of fame: Ludwig Boltzmann (1844–1906)
Nationality: German

Ludwig Boltzmann was big and bearded and miserable. Naturally he wasn't born that way any more than some teachers are born strict or some scientists are born boring. But Ludwig did once say that since he was born on Ash Wednesday and missed the Mardi Gras festival, he was always going to be unhappy. And so it proved. If you have hankies to spare, prepare to make them soggy...

Ludwig's mum and dad were rich and the boy was bright at maths. He went to university and did so well he became a professor at the age of 25. By the time he was 28 he'd developed a theory that explains what atoms in a gas get up to. (Atoms are the tiny objects that make up matter.) Imagine letting off a stink bomb in a science lab. What happens, according to Boltzmann's theory, is that the atoms of a smelly substance don't stay still, they drift off and mingle with the air atoms. And that explains why the smell spreads. And entropy increases.

SO WHAT D'YOU THINK OF BOLTZMANN'S THEORY, CHILDREN?

IT STINKS!

IT'S A GAS!

IT'S A LOAD OF GUFF!

Bet you never knew!
1 Boltzmann's theory suggests that it's possible for an ice cream left in a warm room to actually stop melting and start to freeze again ... but it's not very likely. Mind you, if someone sits on your ice cream it's even less likely to re-freeze.

2 Boltzmann wasn't too interested in the wider meanings of his big breakthrough. He didn't have too much time for philosophers and he thought that one famous thinker, Immanuel Kant (1724–1804), was actually playing a joke on his readers.

By 1877 Ludwig had figured out the maths behind entropy. Atoms get muddled because there's more chance of muddle developing than order. There's more chance of the ice cream on a mug of hot chocolate melting than staying cold. There's more chance of the stink bomb stink filling the room than staying in one corner. Now was he right, was he right or was he *right*?

Many scientists thought that he was *wrong*. Ludwig's ideas depended on atoms, but at that time no one had proved that atoms existed and many scientists didn't believe in them. For these scientists, Ludwig's ideas were as welcome as a clothes moth at a fashion show. And it didn't help that Ludwig didn't make friends easily. He looked odd and had a strange, squeaky voice. He was bad tempered and argued a lot, too. Soon, a gang of heartless scientists were queuing up to bully Boltzmann.

Sometimes science can be *worse* than horrible – it can be cruel, too. For 30 years, Ludwig put up with the scorn and sneers of other scientists and became more and more miserable. And soon after Ludwig developed his great theory, his life began to fall apart. His young son died and he was turned down for a top job. One student remembered that Ludwig was so sad you could hear his heart-rending groans out in the street.

Then, in 1900, an obscure clerk in a Swiss office told his girlfriend that he was sure that Ludwig Boltzmann was right about atoms. In 1905 he explained why. The young clerk's name was Albert Einstein (1879–1955) and he used maths to prove beyond doubt that atoms *did* exist.

But Ludwig never read the article. By then he was nearly blind and suffering from splitting headaches. For a while he'd been thought mad and was locked up in a mental hospital. His wife, Henriette, wrote to their daughter, Ida:

Father gets worse every day. I have almost lost any confidence in the future.

Ludwig and his wife went on holiday. Henriette went for a swim and stopped on the way back to collect her husband's suit from the dry cleaners. When she returned to the house, she found that Ludwig had taken his own life. He was 62 years old.

Ludwig Boltzmann once wrote:

I am conscious of being only an individual struggling against the stream of time.

It was a chillingly accurate prediction.

Time had not been on Ludwig's side. If he'd made time to read Einstein's article he might have cheered up a bit. If his wife had got back to the house in time he might not have died. And if Ludwig had lived just a year longer there is no doubt that he would have won the Nobel Prize and been recognized for the genius that he truly was.

OK, you can blow your noses now but don't get too down, readers. The next chapter is all about how we make sense of time and you're sure to have … the Time of Your Life! (Unlike poor Ludwig!)

THE TIME OF YOUR LIFE

Ever noticed how time seems to speed up when you're enjoying yourself? Isn't it incredible that when you're playing your favourite computer game, or surfing the Net with your mates, time simply zips by?! And when you're waiting your turn at the dentist's, listening to that whining drill going neeeeeeeeeeeeee! – time drags on FOR EVER!

The thing is, when you're wrapped up in what you're doing you stop noticing time, and when you're not doing anything you enjoy, you *do* notice it. And that's what this chapter is all about – how we humans and assorted furry friends and plants sense time.

It's a skill, you know. Imagine you're standing on a pavement. There's a giant lorry crashing down the road but it's some way off. You reckon there's enough time to cross. Phew – you make it! Ever wondered why you don't get squished? It's all thanks to your ability to judge time using your brain's built-in timers. But don't take my word for it – just clock these facts!

Terrible time fact file

NAME: The body clock

DON'T BE ALARMED!

IT'S WHAT MAKES YOU TICK!

THE BASIC FACTS:

1 Your body seems to mark time using a small blob of brain cells no larger than a grain of sand. The cells fire signals at a regular rate like a ticking clock.

2 The brain seems to have a built-in time sense. It does vital jobs such as controlling body temperature, feeling hungry and sleeping on roughly a 24-hour cycle.

PUT A WARM JUMPER ON!

EAT SOMETHING!

GO TO BED!

FLEX!

3 As a result your body is at its best in the late afternoon and early evening when your temperature rises and your muscles are at their strongest.

TERRIBLE DETAILS:

In the early hours of the morning the body is at its weakest. Heart attacks and death are more likely at this time.

FRET! WORRY!

Bet you never knew!

Fancy being shut away in a gloomy cave without daylight or even a clock? That's the fate of volunteers in experiments to find out how the body copes without time clues. In 1989, Stefania Follini moved into "Lost Cave" in New Mexico, USA. She lived there for 18 weeks and, without knowing it, began following a 28-hour day. After six weeks she lost all sense of time and began to stay awake for 30 hours at a stretch. The long days didn't seem to do her any harm but she reported feeling sad and tried to cheer herself up by chatting to mice and frogs.

> OK, SO THAT'S ENOUGH ABOUT ME, WHAT D'YOU GUYS LIKE TO GET UP TO?

I guess the experiment shows that the body needs light and dark to re-set its clock and, as you can find out below, the brain has ways of sensing light.

Terrible expressions

A scientist says: Do you say…?

I'M INTO CIRCADIAN RHYTHMS…

WOW! GIVE ME FIVE! I'M INTO RHYTHM AND THE CIRCADIANS ARE A COOL GROUP!

Well, I hope your circadian rhythms are reaching their peak right now ... because it's quiz time!

Body-time quiz time

1 The brain senses light and produces a substance that makes you feel sleepy in the dark. But during long dark Arctic winters people often can't sleep. What's this condition called?

a) Bug eye.   **b)** Big eye.   **c)** Big head.

2 What's the name of the part of the brain that senses light and makes a sleepy substance that sends you to sleep at night?

b) The pineal gland.

a) The pineapple gland.

c) The peanut gland.

3 Besides the circadian rhythm, the body runs on other cycles that scientists don't fully understand. How often do we reach our peak of germ-fighting powers?

a) Once a week.   **b)** Every ten years.   **c)** Once a month.

4 What's it called when the body's circadian rhythm gets out of sync with daylight after a long flight?

a) Gut lag.

b) Old lag.

c) Jet lag.

And while we're talking about jet lag, if you suffer from the condition you might be interested in a treatment that really seems to work. The travel book below is based on one man's real-life experience.

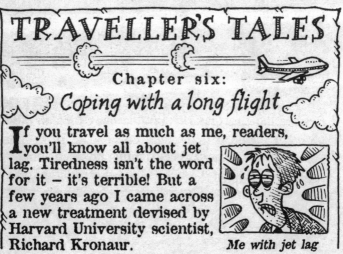

TRAVELLER'S TALES

Chapter six:
Coping with a long flight

If you travel as much as me, readers, you'll know all about jet lag. Tiredness isn't the word for it – it's terrible! But a few years ago I came across a new treatment devised by Harvard University scientist, Richard Kronaur.

Me with jet lag

Richard used pulses of bright light to re-set my body clock. Sounds weird – but it works!

And all I had to do was avoid morning sun on my flight from the USA to England.

That's when I hit upon the idea of wearing welder's goggles. When I arrived at Heathrow Airport, I was very flattered by the attention I was getting. Maybe folks thought I was a movie star! I was smiling and waving until I got arrested by the security guards for looking like a shady character.

Stagger a scientist

Next time you see a scientist, tip-toe up to him or her and tap them on the shoulder…

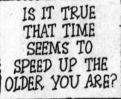

IS IT TRUE THAT TIME SEEMS TO SPEED UP THE OLDER YOU ARE?

ER…

Answer: Yes, or as a scientist might say "probably". Older people grumble that the years roll by faster and faster. Perhaps as a person gets older their brain slows and everything that happens seems faster in comparison, so they think that time is passing more quickly.

31

In one test people listened to two sets of beats and had to decide which one was faster. Children did better at judging the difference between faster beats and older people did better with the slower beats. Perhaps children have faster brains and feel time is passing more slowly than older people. Of course, this explains why children claim science lessons last for ever whilst their elderly teachers think the lessons are too short…

Bet you never knew!
Speedy creatures like flies may see time passing even more slowly than children. Some scientists think that when a fly watches TV, its brain works so fast to put together an image of what's going on that it can actually make out the dark bits in between the TV pictures. A TV shows 25 still pictures a second and our dull plodding brains put them together to see a moving picture and miss the boring dark bits – but flies may not.

Mind you, many animals and plants – even vegged-out potatoes – are better at telling the time than some people. In fact, you can even use them as clocks! We'll be back after the commercial break…

THE HORRIBLE SCIENCE

Old Curiosity Clock Shop

(PET DEPARTMENT)

BORED OF YOUR TIRED—OUT TICK—TOCK?
WHY NOT INVEST IN A *LIVING* TIME—TELLING PET?!

THE OYSTER CLOCK

Guaranteed to open its shell for up to four minutes every hour as long as the tide is high! Mind—boggling moon sensors pick up the pull of the moon's gravity that causes tides and tells your oyster clock when the tide is high. Yes, with this *pearl* of a clock – the world is your oyster!

THE SMALL PRINT: If you get bored of your clock you can always slurp up its insides with a nice garlic sauce!

THE FRUIT—FLY ALARM CLOCK

Finding it hard to get up in the mornings? Why not try the fruit—fly alarm clock? These little bugs manage to emerge for their first flight at dawn – even if they're kept in the dark and their parents and parents' parents, and so on (15 sets of parents here) never saw daylight either!

THE SMALL PRINT: You'll enjoy being woken by the fruit flies crawling up your nostrils, dying in your tea and practising aqua-aerobics in your cornflakes but don't ask us to catch them – we're outta here!

OK! OK! I'M GETTING UP!!!!!!!

EEK! TIME TO MAKE SOME MORE TOAST!
BUZZ!

INTO BUGS? YOU'LL GET A BUZZ FROM THE HONEY-BEE CLOCK!

Leave out marmalade at a certain time each morning and the bees will come round to inspect it at the same time each day, regular as clockwork.

THE SMALL PRINT: And best of all they're at a price that won't sting your pocket – even if they will sting the rest of your body.

INTO GARDENING?

Let our multi-plant clock tell you what time it is...

GOOD MORNING!
GOOD DAY!
GOOD EVENING!

- Spotted cat's ear opens at 6 am.
- Passion flowers open at noon.
- Evening primroses open at 6 pm.

They smell nice and come at a price you won't sneeze at!

NEED TO FIND OUT A FEW MORE TIMES?

May we recommend the one and only potato clock. It may look like an ordinary, boring potato but in fact the "eyes" produce more oxygen gas promptly at 7 am, noon and 6 pm and give out

WHAT'S THE TIME, LOVE?

6 O'CLOCK!

less oxygen gas at night. And get this — they even do it when they're kept in steady light and have no way of telling what time it is!

THE SMALL PRINT: Guaranteed free of silicon chips (but it has got lots of potato chips).

A QUICK NOTE TO THE SCIENTIFICALLY CURIOUS – So you're itching to know how these clocks work? Oh dear – scientists aren't too sure. It may be because some genes switch on and off over time. Genes are chemical instructions made from DNA, the chemical blueprint in living cells that tells them how and when to grow. If DNA can tell children when to turn into teenagers, it can do anything...

Well, as you've just found out, we humans are quite good at keeping track of time but to do it well we really need a clock. And it's much the same thing with longer lengths of time, like weeks and months and years. With them it helps if you have a diary or calendar handy. So why not make space in your diary to read the next chapter?

KILLER CALENDARS

So you think a calendar is something with a nice picture of a kitten on that you buy your granny as a present? Well, you're right – but it's also something that people have racked their brains over and argued over and even killed each other for!

Let's find out how all this calendar fuss began
Even long ago, long before anyone had invented bicycles, indoor toilets or television, people needed to keep track of the days and seasons. In those far-off days your ancestors wore skins, lived in caves and walked around with their knuckles dragging on the ground. And they were keen to know when winter would end, and when there'd be more mammoths to hunt.

Humans probably did find ways to measure time. How? We asked Ug, the intelligent cave-person:

- In summer the sun rises towards the north-east and sets towards the north-west. The days are long and the sun feels hot.

- In spring and autumn the sun rises in the east and sinks to the west. The midday sun is lower than in the summer.

- In winter the sun rises in the south-east and sets in the south-west. The days are short and cold. And I bet cave-people had to wear their sensible thermal underwear. That's right, itchy-scratchy fashion-disaster mammoth-fur underpants!

There are four special days to mark the passing year…

- The summer solstice is the longest day (usually 21 June)*. On that day the noon sun reaches its highest point in the year.
- The winter solstice is the shortest day (usually 21 December)*. The noon sun is now at its lowest point in the year.
- The equinoxes in the spring and autumn (21 March and 21 September) are when day and night are equal in length.

* If you happen to be reading this in the southern half of the Earth these two dates are the other way round.

Now you might be wondering why the sun bothered to make the days different lengths. I mean, was it some kind gesture to help those thicko cave-people sort out the correct time of year?

In fact, it's all down to the fact that the Earth is spinning at an embarrassingly wonky angle…

The Earth whizzes round the sun, taking one year to make the trip.

This means that the northern and southern halves of the Earth take it in turns to lean towards the sun. And that's why when it's winter in Lapland it's summer in Australia…

And people soon figured out that we've had a full year when the sun is at exactly the same point in the sky at noon as it was the previous year…

But we humans want to measure shorter lengths of time than years. I mean, just imagine the terrible results of just having years! Buses and trains would only run once a year, you'd only get one holiday a year and certain members of your family really *would* spend a year in the bathroom.

Fortunately, nature provides a way of cutting the year into smaller bits. Know what it is? I'll give you a clue: you don't have to ask for the moon … but it helps!

Yes, the moon circles the Earth ROUGHLY once a month – you can watch the moon's progress as it seems to change shape from a crescent to a circle and then back again. Clever old moon!

Dare you discover ... how the moon changes shape?

What you need:
The crescent moon (it's up there somewhere!)
A calendar or diary
A compass

What you do:
1 Note down which direction the horns of the crescent are pointing...
2 Look at the crescent moon in about two weeks' time.

What do you notice?
a) The horns are pointing in the opposite direction!
b) The horns are pointing in the same direction.
c) The horns are pointing upwards like a giant smiley face.

Special extra bonus point for clued-up calendar counters. There are a couple of days when the moon can't be seen, followed by what people call the "new moon". So what the heck's going on?

a) The moon moves too far from the Earth for us see it properly.

b) The position of the moon means that it gets no sunlight – so we can't see it.

c) The moon is only out during the day – and it's hard to see.

Answer: c) Daylight is normally too bright for the moon to show up.

OK, so the moon zooms around the Earth and you can be sure what it's up to and when the new moon will appear. So it sounds a real cool idea to use the appearance of the new moon to start a month. Well, early people probably thought so…

Possibly the world's earliest calendar proved horribly fatal for a French eagle 13,000 years ago. Scientists have found an eagle bone with strange markings that could be a record of the changing moon.

Of course, other scientists disagree, violently claiming that it's just a load of grotty old scratches…

But now for a deeply shocking announcement … *ahem!*

For thousands of years people used the moon to measure months. The moon told them when to plant and harvest crops and when to pay taxes. But all these millions of people were doing things on the *wrong* days: the moon had fooled them, cheated them, hoodwinked them, deceived them and made them look as daft as trying to fight a tiger armed only with a pair of false teeth. And here's why...

HA HA HA!
MOON MONTHS
DON'T FIT INTO
THE SUN YEAR!

In the year 2000, the Earth took 365 days, five hours, 48 minutes and 45 seconds to go round the sun, and the moon took 29 days, 12 hours, 44 minutes and 2.9 seconds to go round the Earth. And that means – as they found in ancient China and Greece and Arizona and lots of other places – that if you try to fit 12 moon months into a sun year you're left with a few days over. So your calendar is going to be out by that number of days each year.

Well, you've got to do something with the spare days. And so it was that people like the Babylonians (who lived in the land now known as Iraq), the Greeks and the Romans all ended up slotting the extra days into extra months every few years. Sounds complicated? You bet!

I could tell you all about the many different types of calendar that developed in different parts of the world over thousands of years. But I'm not going to because...

a) You might not be interested.
b) This book would be 1,596 pages long and only read by geeky calendar nerds like Norbert.

So instead I'm going to tell you about the amusingly odd bits…

WHAT CAN HE MEAN?

Amusingly odd calendar facts

1 Religious calendars for Christians, Jews, Muslims and Hindus are still based on the moon. This is why Easter Sunday is officially the first Sunday after the first full moon after the spring equinox.

2 There is probably no scientific reason why a week should last seven days. It seems that in ancient Babylon people quite fancied the number seven and so it's remained.

3 One of the earliest references to the calendar was in a poem by Greek poet Hesiod in 800 BC. The poet lists all the work he had to do during the year in order to tell off his lazy brother for not doing any. Yep, lazy brothers are not a modern invention.

4 In the ancient Aztec calendar there's a cycle of 52 years, at the end of which time was believed to die. In order to stop the world ending, Aztec priests would rip out the beating heart of a victim and burn it in a fire.

Rotten Roman time reckoning

The ancient Roman calendar belonged to priests. No one else was allowed to see the calendar until 304 BC. Then the rule was relaxed after a brave Roman rebel stole a copy of the calendar and showed it to the people.

> *Bet you never knew!*
> *The Romans invented the month names September, October, November and December in 753 BC. The names meant "seventh month", "eighth month" and so on – very imaginative, I DON'T think! "But hold on!" I hear you exclaim. "Surely September is the ninth month, not the seventh!" Well, the Romans switched to a 12-month calendar 50 years later, but carried on using the old names of the months even though they were wrong. And we're still doing it!*

But the Romans had a worse calendar problem. Right from the start the priests could add extra months to the year whenever it suited them. If this custom existed today there would be terrible results at work ... and school.

SORRY, KIDS, THERE'S NO HOLIDAY – THE HEAD'S JUST INVENTED ANOTHER MONTH!

GROAN!

Jules rools OK

Thanks to the priests adding extra months to some years, by 46 BC the calendar was out of step with the seasons. People weren't sure when to bring in the harvest or pay taxes.

But when the going gets tough, the tough get going. And no one was a tougher go-getter than superstar General, and all round big-head, Julius Caesar (100–44 BC).

What's he saying?

We've got to leap every four years.

I'm feeling jumpy already!

One month will be named "July" after my lovely self.*

Now he wants to be called "Julie".

*August was later named after Caesar's equally big-headed great-nephew, Augustus (63 BC – 14 AD).

The new calendar *seemed* to tick along just fine. But there was a problem – the year turned out to be 11 minutes longer than the time the Earth took to go round the sun. Now that doesn't sound too bad. I mean, what's 11 minutes between friends – huh? Trouble is the next year the calendar was out by *another* 11 minutes and so on. And if you don't have a calculator handy I'd better say 11 minutes a year equals ONE WHOLE DAY every 134 years – or 11 days in 1,500 years. So it wasn't long before Christmas and Easter and everyone's birthday ended up on the wrong days!

Over the next 1,300 years quite a few scientists sussed that the days were wrong. And the experts passed on the bad news to the Pope. (As boss of the Church, the Pope was the only man with the power to put things right.) For some reason some of these experts had silly names ... for example, there were Notker the Stammerer, Notker the Peppercorn and Notker the thick-lipped (all no relations).

But the most famous expert of the lot was a monk named Roger Bacon (1214–1292) – or Friar Bacon to use his official job title. Now I could tell you a lot about Roger but I'm not going to because I've just discovered a long-lost book about him by his best friend! Oh hold on, it might be a forgery…

Roger Bacon – the monk behind the myth
by Friar Egg

"Friar Bacon" – just saying that name makes me think of breakfast – why didn't he have a sensible name like me? But then people say I'm not the brightest monk in the bunch. The other monks call me "Half-cracked Egg" – I can't think why!

ME

Anyway, that's enough of me – I want to tell you about my monkish mate Roger!

Our boss, the Prior, didn't like Rog. And Rog didn't like him – always arguing they were. I mean, Rog reckoned he knew how to teach the young monks better than anyone and the boss

THE PRIOR

didn't like that. So Roger was picked on and given all the rotten jobs no one else wanted to do. Naturally I gave Rog moral support by not getting in his way when he was scrubbing out the toilets.

PONG!

Then one day – oh, it must have been in 1266, Rog got a letter that put a grin on his face. He heard that an old mate of his named Guy had just been elected Pope. And guess what – this Guy wanted Rog to tell him all his ideas about everything! But then Rog realized he hadn't written anything down – he'd been too busy cleaning out the pigpen and cutting the other monks' toenails.

Dear Rog
Please tell me everything!
Guy

Well, Rog got to work and this time the boss didn't dare stop him – not when the Pope commands and all that. And after two years of working night and day Rog finished it – it was a weighty work! I know, I dropped it on my toe – ouch!

ARGH!

"What shall I call it, idiot-features?" asked Rog.

He always used this friendly tone of address with me – me being his mate and all that.

"Well, it's a major work," I said, ruefully rubbing my pet corn.

THUMP!

"Love the title!" shouted Rog, giving me a friendly punch and sending me sprawling.

And that's what he called it – "Major Work".

Now, I can't say exactly what was in it 'cos it's got lots of pages and no pictures and I haven't started it yet. But I know that Rog was a bit rude about the Church for letting the calendar go all out of sync. Rog said that the calendar's 11 minutes out a year - and that means that Easter is always on the wrong day.

Anyway, Rog gave a copy of the book to his servant, John, and sent him to Rome to give it to the Pope. Well, when John got back he said it was a tough journey and he nearly got robbed a few times. But he made it to Rome in the end. Trouble was the Pope had died and no one else wanted to read Roger's book.

HE'S DEAD!

Now, my mate Rog, he never gave up without a fight. He wrote to all the top people in the Church to tell them where they were going wrong about the calendar and everything else. And boy did they take notice of him! They took SIZZLE! so much notice of him that they locked him up in prison for 15 years.

By the time they let him out he was a frazzled friar, or you might say a bit of a burnt-out Bacon. Sadly he died soon after and everyone's forgotten him except me - his true monk-mate - Friar Egg.

Of course, Bacon was right and even the Church wasn't powerful enough to change the way the Earth moved. By 1582 the calendar was almost two weeks wrong and things were getting serious – or should I say too darn silly for words…

HAPPY EASTER, YOUR HOLINESS!

BUT IT'S CHRISTMAS, YOUR MAJESTY!

Bet you never knew!
1 The year had been accurately measured by several scientists outside Europe. Arab scientist Abu Allah Mohammed Ibn Jabir al-Battani (850–929) used astronomical observations to get it right to within 28 seconds.
2 In central Asia, Ullagh Beg (1394–1449) was a prince with an interest in astronomy and an odd ambition to become a science teacher (how weird can you get!). He set up his own university so he could teach science, and spent a fortune building his own observatory so he could study the stars. In fact, Ullagh proved to be a star star-gazer who measured the year to within 25 seconds of its true length. Sadly, his son was less of a star. He plotted against his scientist dad and sliced open his head with a sword. That wasn't a "slice" thing to do – was it?

Anyway, back in Europe one of the world's greatest unsung heroes was about to make his appearance. This person should be more famous than Mickey Mouse but sadly no one can even decide *what his name was*…

Hall of fame: Luigi Lilio otherwise known as Aloysius Lilius (that's his name in Latin) (1510–1576) Nationality: Italian

If you just said "Luigi who?" I don't blame you. In fact, I bet that 99.99999% of the readers of this book have never heard of him! Some people are incredibly famous for doing nothing important – kicking a football, singing a few songs, acting in movies – but so what? Luigi Lilio is unbelievably *un-famous* for doing something STUPENDOUS. Something so incredibly important that it affects every day of our lives.

He invented our modern calendar.

And here's how he did it…

Luigi was a retired doctor and university teacher living quietly in southern Italy when one day in the early 1570s he had an incredible idea:

IT'S TIME TO GET THE CALENDAR RIGHT!

In a rush of excitement the old doctor sat down and wrote down his brilliant brainwave in a book. Then he packed up his belongings and travelled to Rome to tell the Pope. Soon afterwards he died.

And that, you might well think, should have been that. After all, if they didn't listen to brainy Bacon why should anyone listen to laid-out Luigi especially seeing as he was dead. But Luigi had a secret weapon: his brother, Antonio. And Antonio battled to get the Pope and other important people to take his brother's plan seriously. At last, in 1578, he succeeded.

As popes go, Gregory XIII (1502–1585) was not exactly *Top of the Popes*. He taxed the people heavily and spent the money on big celebrations and grand buildings whilst poor folk went hungry. But he did sort out the calendar mess. Or more accurately he set up a group led by German astronomer Christopher Clavius (1537–1612) to do the job for him. And they backed Luigi Lilio's plan.

You see, Lilio's plan had one big advantage: it was simple and it was common sense. Er – hold on that's actually two. We'd best let Luigi speak for himself…

Er – can you explain this, Norbert?

Luigi's plan worked! Well, not quite, as it was still one day out every 3,300 years, but hey – who cares! Well, obviously some people do...

TUT, TUT –
ONE WHOLE
DAY!

Gradually the new calendar spread throughout Europe and America. In parts of what is now Belgium and the Netherlands the authorities decided to miss the extra ten days over Christmas. So Christmas was cancelled! No doubt children cried and mean-minded parents secretly rejoiced. By 1949, when China adopted the calendar it had swept the entire world and you can be sure that it was named after the one person who made it all possible. That's right ... good ol' Pope Gregory!

It's called the "Gregorian Calendar" and not the "Lilian Calendar" because Luigi was dead and buried. In fact the Pope's office even lost their original copy of Luigi's book. So remember folks – if you want to be dead famous, it's a bad idea to be too dead before your wonderful ideas are taken up by important people who become famous instead of you.

HEE, HEE!

Dating disasters
Of course, the calendar can tell us what day of the year it is – but it doesn't keep track of the years. The idea of numbering the years was invented by an obscure priest

named Dionysius Exguus (500–560). But everyone called him "Little Dennis" either because he was a bit lacking in the height department or he didn't have much to say for himself.

Anyway, Dennis invented the term "AD" (now known as CE or Common Era). AD stands for *anno Domini*, "the year of our Lord". It was meant to number the years since Jesus was born, but it didn't. And why not?

1 Today's historians think that Jesus was born in 4 BC. Oh, what's wrong now, Norbert?

2 Dennis started off with year one and not year zero – he can't be blamed for this since the idea of a number zero didn't reach Europe (from India via Arabia) for another 200 years.

A terribly shocking thought

Er – hold on! I've just thought of something! That means history teachers and history books have been wrong about dates for over 2,000 years! Even the dates in this book are wrong! It means that the real Millennium celebrations should have been in 1996 and the WHOLE WORLD missed the big day! OOPS!

Bet you never knew!
You may have heard of the Chinese practice of naming years after animals – the year of the rat, the year of the tiger and so on. But did you know that the year you were born in is supposed to give you certain qualities? Good teachers are born in the year of the monkey – but younger readers are advised not to share this fact with their educators…

But anyway, the calendar was sorted. Mind you, some people went on inventing their own calendars with terrible results. I mean, look what happened in France in 1792! After the French Revolution in 1789 the new leaders wanted to change the calendar to something they thought was more logical. No doubt the papers were full of it – especially when things went terribly wrong…

The Daily Revolution

5 April 1794

CROOKED CALENDAR-CHANGER GETS CHOP!

All Paris turned out today to see Philippe Fabre D'Eglantine lose his head. The potty ex-poet hit the big time two years ago when he backed a scatter-brained scheme to change the calendar.

The new calendar was introduced by law and made the year ten months and the day ten hours. But a bid to make the week ten days long flopped after people complained about getting one day off in ten. Fabre's enemies said he stole money and took bribes. His career came a cropper and he faced the chopper!

At the execution the time-tinkering traitor was calm and kept his head right until the end. As time ran out he handed poems to the crowd. Typical author – anything for a bit of free publicity!

The new calendar was scrapped in 1805 but by then most people had been ignoring it for years. The idea of changing the clock time was even less successful: it had as much chance of catching on as a wig in a hurricane. And now we're on the subject of clocks it's time to discover some crazy old timers…

No, I meant the time-keeping machines in the next chapter!

CRAZY CLOCKS

Where would we be without clocks? You wind up your clock – (well, the old-fashioned type) and then it winds you up by waking you up in the morning and reminding you how late you are. But clocks are crucial and this chapter explains why…

Stop the clock!

Our whole lives are bound up with measuring time in halting hours, meandering minutes and swiftly speeding seconds. I mean – can you name one sport that doesn't depend on clocks to time speeds or the length of a game? Yep – you even need a clock for snail racing…

… AND AFTER A SLUGGISH START, MR. MOLLUSC WINS BY A FRACTION OF… AN HOUR. ER… 35 MINUTES, ACTUALLY.

You may like to know that the hour, the second and the minute were invented in Babylon over 4,000 years ago. Mind you, without a clock, hours, seconds and minutes are as useful as a diving suit in the desert – but around this time (3500 BC) the world's first time-measuring device came out of the shadows. Some people still have one in their gardens. Don't go away – we'll be back after this commercial break…

For an extra ₤999,999.99 we'll put ancient Egyptian picture writing on your obelisk just like the original. Then everyone can read about your heroic deeds and the battles you've won!

THE SMALL PRINT – Since the Earth's orbit round the sun is an ellipse (like a squashed circle) and not a circle, the sun takes longer to cross the sky on some days than others. And this means your clock won't always be accurate.

Terrible expressions

A time expert announces:

I HAVE A HUGE GNOMON IN MY GARDEN...

Do you say...?

OH YEAH – MY AUNTIE BERYL'S GOT MILLIONS OF GNOMES IN HER GARDEN!

Answer: Only if you want to upset our expert and that might be bad for your 'elf – I mean health. For your information, a gnomon (no-mon) is an upright object that casts a shadow to tell the time – like our obelisk.

Message to younger readers

What's that? Your penny-pinching parents won't buy you an obelisk? Oh shame! Oh well, why not make your own sundial? OK, it's not as grand as the one in the advert but it's cheap and cheerful and you don't need any slaves to build it! And when you've made the sundial there's another clock to make too...

Dare you discover ... how to make your own clock?

1 The sundial

What you need:

A piece of card
A torch
Some scissors
A ruler

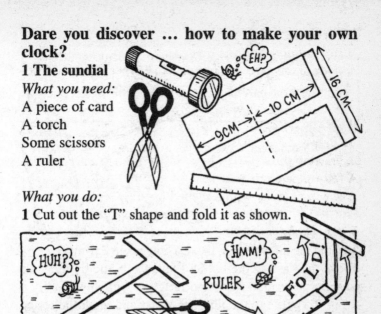

What you do:

1 Cut out the "T" shape and fold it as shown.

2 Place the ruler over the flat part of the shape.

3 Darken the room and switch on the torch. Move the torch in an arc like the sun rising and moving across the sky.

You should notice:

The lower the sun (WHOOPS, I mean torch), the longer the shadow. In most parts of the Earth the midday sun appears lower in the sky in the winter and higher in the summer – so a sundial can also tell you what time of year it is.

2 The water clock

Historical note

A clock of this type was invented in Egypt around 1350 BC. The Greeks called it a clepsydra or "water thief".

What you need:
An empty 2-litre plastic bottle
A drawing pin
A felt-tip pen
A watch or clock with a second hand

What you do:
1 Using the drawing pin, make a hole about 2.5 cm (1 inch) above the base of the bottle. Place the bottle by the sink to avoid unwanted floods and friction with your family.
2 Fill the bottle to the top with water and mark the water level. Time a minute. Mark the new water level as the bottle empties through the hole into the sink. Time another minute and carry on until you get bored.
3 Read the rest of this book in between marking minutes.

You should notice:
The minute marks get closer together as the water gets lower and empties more slowly from the bottle. Of course, a cold night might freeze the clock and dirt could block the hole.

Wherever clocks were installed they began to take over peoples' lives. Ancient Greek thinker Aristotle (384–322 BC) complained that when people went to the theatre they didn't follow the play because they were watching the public water clock. In Athens, people used a huge water clock to find out when boring politicians ran over the time allowed for their speeches.

In 100 BC an ancient Greek wrote…

When I was young there was no other clock for me but my belly. For me it was the best and most accurate clock, at its call we ate, unless there was nothing to eat…

He added that since those funny newfangled sundial thingies had become popular people ate their lunch when the sundial told them it was lunchtime, and that meant they got really hungry whilst they were waiting. Do you know the feeling?

Bet you never knew!
The first clocks appeared in the 1280s. No one knows who invented them but they were so inaccurate they only had one hand – to count the hours.
The key to building a clock that could tell the right time turned out to be a neat little gizmo…

THUD!

RATTLE!

CLUNK! CLANK!

Terrible expressions

A clock expert says:

I NEED AN ESCAPEMENT

Do you say...?

WHY, WHO'S AFTER YOU?

Bet you never knew!
From the 1650s the time-keeping part of the clock was a swinging weight (or "pendulum") or a wheel that rocked to and fro under the control of a small spring. Both moved at a regular rate. Of course these old timers are valuable antiques now and not to be confused with old-time humans who are still into rock and swing.

Clock this!

1 Before the first pendulum clock, astronomers timed stars moving across the sky by forcing children to swing pendulums and count the exact number of swings. In those days "having a go on the swings" was far less popular.

2 The power for a pendulum clock comes from weights that slowly descend in stages controlled by the swinging pendulum. This means that the traditional grandfather clock doesn't work in space, as there's no gravity to pull the weights down.

WHAT TIME IS IT?

I HAVEN'T A CLUE – THE CAPTAIN INSISTED ON BRINGING HIS GRANDFATHER CLOCK!

3 And the sea is just as bad. The inventor of both the pendulum and the spring clocks, Dutch super-scientist Christiaan Huygens (1629–1695), tried for 20 years to build a clock that would keep good time at sea. But to keep time a pendulum needs to swing at a fixed rate and that's hard when the ship is being tossed around like a rubber duck in a paddling pool. And springs and other metal parts were affected by heat and cold.

Well, that's tough. As you're about to find out, seafarers didn't just need accurate clocks to find out what time it was, they needed them to find out where they were at sea. And bad time-keeping could prove dangerously deadly, as we'll see in the next chapter... Don't be late!

THE WRONG TIME AND PLACE

Finding out where you are at sea is a PROBLEM. Once you're out of sight of land there's not much to put on your map except a pretty blue colour and the word "SEA", so you need a device to tell you where you are.

That device proved to be the clock and Norbert is about to explain how to use it. I ought to say that when he isn't at home glued to his computer screen, our geeky pal, Norbert, enjoys a bit of messing about in his dinghy…

How to find out how far east or west you are at sea in three ever-so-easy stages with Norbert

You set an accurate clock to the correct time.

THAT'S 08.01 AND 35 SECONDS TO BE PRECISE.

You set sail…

WHEN THE SUN IS OVERHEAD IT'S NOON – OR 1200 HOURS.

The clock tells Norbert the time at the port.

IT'S 11.59 AM BACK THERE.

And the overhead sun means it's 1200 hours on board Norbert's dinghy.

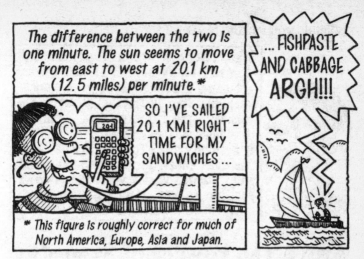

The difference between the two is one minute. The sun seems to move from east to west at 20.1 km (12.5 miles) per minute.*

... FISHPASTE AND CABBAGE ARGH!!!

SO I'VE SAILED 20.1 KM! RIGHT — TIME FOR MY SANDWICHES ...

* This figure is roughly correct for much of North America, Europe, Asia and Japan.

Sounds simple. But as I said, back in the olden days, clocks didn't keep good time at sea. So inventors looked at other ideas even if they were a bit daft...

Loopy longitude methods

We've invited the inventors to show off their plans. And Norbert is going to explain their drawbacks ... ready, guys?

1 The Telescope Helmet

INVENTOR: Italian mega-genius Galileo Galilei

DATE: around 1611

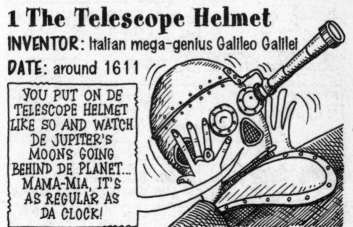

YOU PUT ON DE TELESCOPE HELMET LIKE SO AND WATCH DE JUPITER'S MOONS GOING BEHIND DE PLANET... MAMA-MIA, IT'S AS REGULAR AS DA CLOCK!

What do you reckon, Norbert?

Well, I suppose it's a good idea but I'm not really sure if it will work. You see, it's hard to spot a planet when the ship is tossing about in the ocean. I tried it once and jammed the telescope in my earhole! And if it's cloudy then it's impossible! Also the time taken for light to reach us from Jupiter varies with the planet's position so you can't set your clock by it. Fascinating stuff, though!

2 The Powder of Sympathy

INVENTOR: Sir Kenelm Digby

DATE: 1687

YELP!

A) I WOUND A DOG LIKE SO...

WHIMPER!

B) I STAY AT HOME AND SEND THE DOG ON A LONG SEA VOYAGE!

C) EVERY DAY AT NOON I SPRINKLE MY POWDER ON THE DOG'S BLOOD-STAINED BANDAGE.

HOWL!

D) THE DOG FEELS THE PAIN AND HOWLS — AND THIS TELLS THE SHIP'S CREW WHEN IT'S NOON AT HOME!

68

I've spent the last eight hours looking through all my time books and the Internet for this powder and I am forced to conclude that it does not exist! I think this idea must be a hoax!

An urgent warning from the author Don't try this at home, readers. It's cruelty to animals and may result in a long prison sentence and a badly bitten backside!

3 The signal-ships plan

INVENTORS: William Whiston and Humphrey Ditton

DATE: 1713

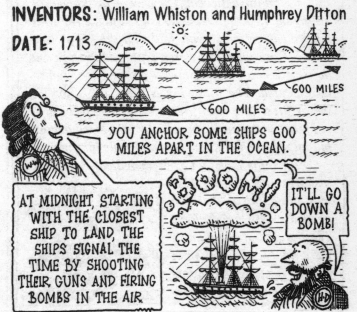

600 MILES

600 MILES

YOU ANCHOR SOME SHIPS 600 MILES APART IN THE OCEAN.

AT MIDNIGHT, STARTING WITH THE CLOSEST SHIP TO LAND, THE SHIPS SIGNAL THE TIME BY SHOOTING THEIR GUNS AND FIRING BOMBS IN THE AIR

BOOM!

IT'LL GO DOWN A BOMB!

Oh dear, oh dear, oh dear! I've never heard of such twaddle! I've done a lot of digging out facts and found out that oceans are too deep to anchor in. In bad weather guns and bombs wouldn't be heard or seen. And it would prove difficult to keep the ships supplied with food. I'm afraid this idea is a bit of a "bomber", ha ha!

Bet you never knew!

In 1707 a fleet of English ships was sailing home after a battle. Admiral Sir Clowdisley Shovell was looking forward to a hero's welcome when a sailor warned him that the fleet was further west than the ship's captain believed. They were in danger of hitting the rocks of the Scilly Isles! But the Admiral backed his captains who said that the sailor was wrong. Crew members weren't allowed to work out the ship's course and Shovell ordered the man to be executed. The following evening the ships hit the Scillies. One man from Shovell's ship lived to tell the tale. Admiral Shovell also staggered ashore but an old woman killed him and stole his ring.

Three ships sank and 2,000 men died. They were lost at sea after losing their way at sea. But all they had needed was a good clock. The pride of England's navy went to the bottom of the sea because its leaders didn't know the right time.

ERK!

EEK!

ARGH!

Stunned by the disaster, in 1714 the British Parliament offered a reward of £20,000 for anyone who could invent a way to solve the problem of measuring longitude to an accuracy of 48.27 km (30 miles).

IMPORTANT NOTE

In those days, £20,000 was worth a fortune. In today's money it would be about TEN MILLION POUNDS. It was the greatest prize in the history of science.

Bet you never knew!
Lines of longitude are imaginary north-south lines that mark off how far east or west you are on a map.

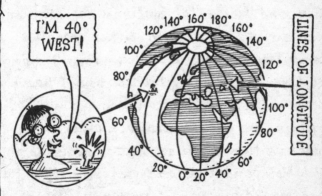

The prize looked hard to win. As Norbert explained, the ideas put around at the time had less chance of making it than a balloon in a pin factory. But there was still the hope of building a clock that kept time at sea. And one man was determined to do it and win the prize.

Hall of fame: John Harrison (1693–1776)
Nationality: British

When John was a young lad he fell ill and his parents placed a watch on his pillow so he could listen to the ticking. In those days watches were rare and expensive and the boy was enthralled by this strange machine. He was fascinated by science too and even copied out an entire book of science notes. Now was that dedication – or what?

John's dad was a carpenter and the boy learnt the trade. When he was 19, John built his first wooden clock. It was so finely made that everyone who saw it had to agree that the young man had a special talent for making things. Here's what John's notebook might have looked like…

1726 ~ Pesky things - pendulum clocks! The pendulum metal swells in hot weather and shrinks in the cold. Either way, the pendulum changes length and won't swing to time. Anyway, my brother and I have designed a pendulum containing two metals. The metals hold each other in place as they swell up. And it works! The new pendulum loses just one second a month! I reckon we're onto something here!

It was an incredible achievement! With no training and little money two young men had built the most accurate clock ever known! John decided that he could win the Longitude Prize. But would his skill be enough?

It took John four years to draw up his clock plans and then he went to London to see the Board of Longitude – this was the committee Parliament had set up to award the prize. In London John met Edmond Halley (1656–1742), a leading member of the Board. Halley sent John to see George Graham – the finest watchmaker in London. But what would the expert make of John's plans?

The expert was impressed. John and George Graham talked for ten hours – non-stop! And the watchmaker loaned the young man cash to build his clock. But it took John five more years of work before the clock was ready. No doubt his notebook was full of it…

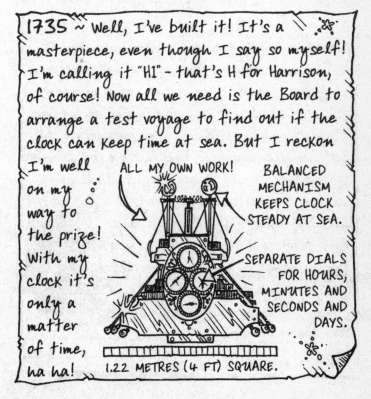

1735 ~ Well, I've built it! It's a masterpiece, even though I say so myself! I'm calling it "H1" – that's H for Harrison, of course! Now all we need is the Board to arrange a test voyage to find out if the clock can keep time at sea. But I reckon I'm well on my way to the prize! With my clock it's only a matter of time, ha ha!

ALL MY OWN WORK!

BALANCED MECHANISM KEEPS CLOCK STEADY AT SEA.

SEPARATE DIALS FOR HOURS, MINUTES AND SECONDS AND DAYS.

1.22 METRES (4 FT) SQUARE.

After months of delay the Board agreed to test the clock by sending it and John on a sea voyage to Lisbon, Portugal. Here's a letter John might have written to his wife, Elizabeth.

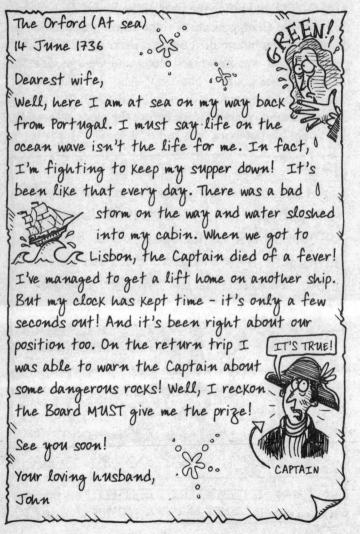

The Orford (At sea)
14 June 1736

Dearest wife,
Well, here I am at sea on my way back from Portugal. I must say life on the ocean wave isn't the life for me. In fact, I'm fighting to keep my supper down! It's been like that every day. There was a bad storm on the way and water sloshed into my cabin. When we got to Lisbon, the Captain died of a fever! I've managed to get a lift home on another ship. But my clock has kept time – it's only a few seconds out! And it's been right about our position too. On the return trip I was able to warn the Captain about some dangerous rocks! Well, I reckon the Board MUST give me the prize!

See you soon!

Your loving husband,
John

GREEN!

IT'S TRUE!

CAPTAIN

But the Board said the test *didn't* count. John should have gone to the *West Indies* – so why did they send him to Lisbon? In any case, you might think John was too honest for his own good. He said the clock needed improving – and he began to build a new one. At least this time the Board gave him some cash up front.

Let's take another peek in that notebook…

1741
Well, that was a mistake and a half! It's taken me four years to build H2 and it's even heavier than H1! It's more accurate and can withstand high and low temperatures.
H2
And yes, the scientists at the Royal Society have tested it by shaking to prove that it can stand up to a voyage. But that's not good enough for me!
I KNOW I CAN DO BETTER!

Once more John began making a new clock. This time the work took even longer. Another EIGHTEEN years in fact!

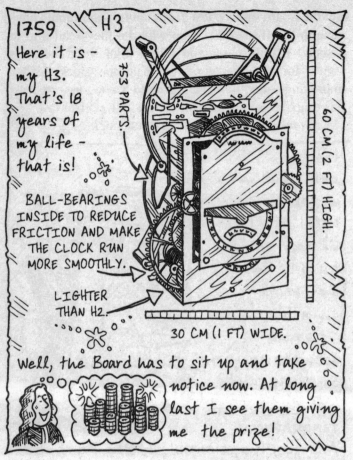

1759 H3

Here it is — my H3. That's 18 years of my life — that is!

753 PARTS.

BALL-BEARINGS INSIDE TO REDUCE FRICTION AND MAKE THE CLOCK RUN MORE SMOOTHLY.

LIGHTER THAN H2.

60 CM (2 FT) HIGH.

30 CM (1 FT) WIDE.

Well, the Board has to sit up and take notice now. At long last I see them giving me the prize!

Meanwhile, the Board had been looking at plans by astronomers to use the moon to find longitude. The idea was to predict when the moon appeared to pass certain stars on certain days as seen from London. Mariners could clock the time when this happened (using a clock they re-set at noon) and compare this to the London time. And they could use the time difference to work out the distance east or west of London.

You might think this is terribly complicated – and you'd be right – but the scientists on the Board liked the idea. They thought it was more scientific than using a humble clock. But John was busy working on yet another clock…

1761

Here it is – H4. Isn't it a little gem?

H4

MY LITTLE BEAUTY!

12.7 CM (5 INCHES).

DIAMOND BEARINGS TO REDUCE FRICTION.

I think it's the most beautiful object in the whole world!

The new clock – the "watch" as John called it – was a miracle. Nothing like it had ever been seen before, and it seemed impossible that such a small thing could measure time with the accuracy the Board demanded. The Board wasn't impressed, but in the end agreed to test the clock on a voyage to the West Indies. By now John was too old to travel and so he waved goodbye to the two most precious things in his life – his watch and his son, William. Here's a letter that William might have sent his father…

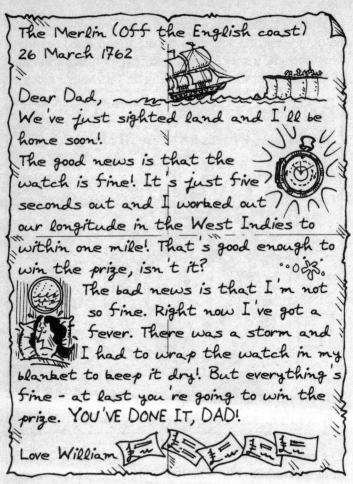

The Merlin (Off the English coast)
26 March 1762

Dear Dad,
We've just sighted land and I'll be home soon!
The good news is that the watch is fine! It's just five seconds out and I worked out our longitude in the West Indies to within one mile! That's good enough to win the prize, isn't it?
The bad news is that I'm not so fine. Right now I've got a fever. There was a storm and I had to wrap the watch in my blanket to keep it dry! But everything's fine - at last you're going to win the prize. YOU'VE DONE IT, DAD!

Love William

Some chance! The Board came up with a new excuse and said that William hadn't tested the watch properly. So he had to take the watch back to the West Indies and do it all over again! And this time Nevil Maskelyne would be there too. Maskelyne was an astronomer and a supporter of the rival moon method. Here's how the papers might have reported the new test…

THE CLOCKMAKER'S TIMES

CRUCIAL CRUNCH CLOCK CRUISE

W. HARRISON

John Harrison is scenting success in his long longitude prize quest. The veteran clockmaker proudly told how his son, William, sailed for a second time to the West Indies, where his "watch" kept near-perfect time.

Rival timer, Nevil Maskelyne botched his observations of the moon after a row with William. "He wasn't exactly over the moon," reported William.

N. MASKELYNE

John Harrison had done everything to win the prize – but *still* the Board dragged its feet. It must have been incredibly, unbelievably frustrating. And then disaster struck. Still smarting from the row with William, Nevil Maskelyne became Astronomer Royal, that's the top British astronomer, and joined the Board. Would he take his revenge on John? Here's John's notebook again…

1766

I've spent 40 years trying to win this prize. I even spent six days showing experts how my watch works - before they took it away and ordered me to build a new one ... from memory! And now this...

This morning, Maskelyne turned up with a gang of men to take away my other clocks. He says the Board wants him to test them. When the workmen laid rough hands on the beautiful wooden cases I was shaking with fear and fury. Then a clumsy oaf drops my H1 in the gutter with a horrible jangling crash. I shuddered to see the work of 40 years jolting and bumping away on the back of a dirty old cart. I'VE HAD IT UP TO HERE! Sorry about the tear stains ... I don't think I'll ever get over this...

By now John was an old man. He couldn't walk or see too well. The only thing that kept him going was the hope that somehow one day he would get justice and win the prize. But Maskelyne claimed that the clocks didn't keep good time. Odd that – they did well enough in all those tests at sea. Meanwhile the astronomer boasted that his charts of the moon's position had solved the longitude problem for good.

Was this the end of John Harrison's dream?

A timely question

John was running out of time – he was 74 years old and not expected to last much longer.

So how do you think his story ends?

Well, let's find out, shall we?

William went to see King George at his castle and told His Majesty about his father's long battle to claim his reward. Surprisingly the King was interested in science and clocks and already knew some of the facts. But he couldn't believe how badly John had been treated.

When William finished his story, His Majesty was visibly moved and turned away muttering, "These people have been cruelly treated."

The King promised to put things right and ordered a new set of tests. The watch kept near-perfect time. In June 1773, Parliament passed a law to award John a generous cash reward.

John was 80 years old and near the end of his life. He never lived to see clocks based on his designs taken in ships all over the world and never knew how many thousands of lives they saved.

Today, millions of visitors come to marvel at John's clocks at the National Maritime Museum, Greenwich. And John Harrison is honoured as the greatest clockmaker of all time.

Of course time's moved on since those days and we must too. So let's get really up to date and check out how time is measured in modern times...

Get ready to say "COR!" rather a lot.

MAKING GOOD TIME

Building a clock that could help you find your location proved to be just the start. Today time is organized and mapped across the whole world and measured with super-accuracy to billionths of a second. And there have been bucket-loads of shiny-new time inventions – like the 24-hour clock.

The terribly confusing 24-hour clock

Can you make sense of the 24-hour clock? That's the one where 5 pm is known as 1700 hours and so on? If you can't, you may like to know who's to blame for it...

Well, here he is now: Sandford Fleming, the great time expert. He's about to make a discovery on a station platform at Bandoran, Ireland in 1876. He's so keen to catch a vital train that he's turned up three hours early. But we'll leave him to discover the terrible truth in his own good time...

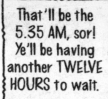

That'll be the 5.35 AM, sor! Ye'll be having another TWELVE HOURS to wait.

Harumph! I'll miss my ferry to England!

The trouble about being in a hurry, sor, is that you never have time for anything important...

SHUT UP!

Sandford spent the next 12 hours trying to think up a way to prevent this kind of maddening misunderstanding. And his simple solution was the 24-hour clock – a clock that made it clear whether the time was morning or afternoon (that's if you can understand it!).

If Sandford had done nothing more in his life than invent the 24-hour clock, he'd have merely changed the lives of millions of people all over the world for ever. But he did MORE, much, much more and that's why he deserves a place in our Horrible Science...

Hall of fame: Sandford Fleming (1827–1915)
Nationality: Scottish-born Canadian

As the ship rolled and tossed and pitched in the mountainous seas, the frightened passengers hugged and prayed. Meanwhile, on the heaving deck, as the freezing spray stung his face and fierce wind tugged his clothes, a youthful scientist calmly measured the wind speed and direction.

It looked like young Sandford Fleming's dream of leaving his native Scotland for Canada had ended before it had begun. He sealed the letter in a bottle and tossed it overboard hoping that someone somewhere would find it and send it to his family. And in fact they did. A few months later the Fleming family learnt of the death of their son in a storm.

Except that he was still alive...

At the last moment the wind had dropped and the ship had made it to Canada. Young Sandford could begin his climb to fame and fortune as a top railway planner. And the secret of his success? Well, you might say it was talent... Sandford was good at his job as a surveyor (someone who maps the route of railways) and he was a talented artist who designed Canada's first postage stamp.

Or you might say that Sandford had energy. I mean this guy never stopped! He belonged to 70 scientific societies, and when he was on a ship he would walk 4.8 km (3 miles) round the ship every day to keep fit. And he later got involved in a project to lay a telegraph cable across the Pacific Ocean – I expect that was light relief.

But I think that Sandford's secret was to do with time. He knew how to make the most of it. He had this idea that he should never waste a second. Even when he wasn't working he was practising his drawing or designing a new kind of roller skate or writing articles about the science of rocks. And when he wasn't striding round a ship he was writing a newspaper for the other passengers.

So time was very important to our pal Sandford, and that's why he was so annoyed about being stuck in a station for 12 hours, and that's why he used the time to think up some seriously scintillating ideas.

The timely time-zones idea

Sandford began to think that the whole world should be divided into time zones based on the spinning of the Earth. It took him two years to work out the details. The idea was that there would be 24 time zones. Each zone would cover 15° of the 360° of longitude or one hour of the sun's passage across the sky. And the time would be the same everywhere in a zone.

Time zones were a great idea and the reason was big and dirty and made an odd puffing sound. No, I'm not talking about your grandpa – it was the steam train! Before time zones, travelling by train was as tricky as cutting a gnat's toenails. Just imagine what TV travel shows would have made of it – that's if they'd had TV in those days!

Here at Buffalo, New York, there are three different railway company times and a separate local time. Which means that...

WE'VE JUST MISSED OUR TRAIN!

Time zones would make it simpler for railway companies to keep their trains running on time. What's more, people could do business abroad by telegraph (and later by phone) more easily because they could work out the time in other countries. So, at last, in 1884, after arguments about where to have the 0° line and where to start the day, Sandford's idea was taken up by the leading nations of the world.

Here's a map showing the time zones. Which one do you live in?

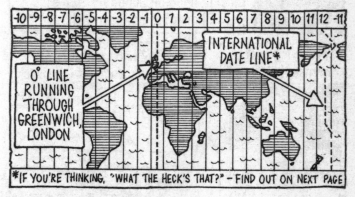

0° LINE RUNNING THROUGH GREENWICH, LONDON

INTERNATIONAL DATE LINE*

*IF YOU'RE THINKING, "WHAT THE HECK'S THAT?" – FIND OUT ON NEXT PAGE

And here's how they work: the 0° line runs through Greenwich, London. East of Greenwich, each time zone is one hour ahead of Greenwich time. As you travel west each time zone is one hour behind Greenwich time.

The really mind-wobbling bit is when you get to the International Date Line. This line is 180° west of Greenwich in the middle of the Pacific Ocean. It's 12 hours ahead of Greenwich going east but 12 hours *behind* Greenwich going west. And that raises the interesting question of what day is it on the Date Line? Can it be two days at once? We've sent Norbert and his dinghy (at great expense) off to investigate.

So that's your answer, folks! On the Date Line, you get two days side-by-side, 24 hours apart. And that's why they call it the "Date Line"!

Terribly weird facts about time zones

1 The International Date Line zigzags to avoid land. One zigzag was drawn on the map to avoid the Morrell and Byers islands near Hawaii – until someone discovered that the islands didn't exist. They were a map-maker's mistake!

2 In the USA, some towns refused to join a time zone. Detroit was close to a line and kept changing its mind about which zone to be in. This meant that the time kept changing too.

3 In 1852, Britain moved from local time to time based on the time at the Royal Observatory in Greenwich. Lots of people were upset at losing their local time and there were big arguments. In Birmingham, scientist Abraham Osler (1808–1903) cunningly re-set a public clock to London time when no one was looking. In Bristol, an old councillor didn't accept the new time. He spent years being 14 minutes late for everything.

The ultimate excuse for being late all your life

Have you ever wanted to be late and get away with it? Yes, just imagine – you could laze about and roll up for things whenever you felt like it! And you could go to bed late and get up late whenever it suited you! Interested? Read on! All you do is smile sweetly and explain:

IMPORTANT AND TERRIBLY URGENT SCIENTIFIC NOTE

Saying this may result in further questioning/torture sessions, so you will need to know what your local time is. This is the time in terms of the sun's position in the sky as opposed to the time zone time that everyone else is trying to follow.

Dare you discover ... what your local time is?

What you need:

A map that shows time zones
A ruler
A pocket calculator

What you do:

1 Find out where the western border of your time zone is.
2 Find out where you are on the map.
3 Using the ruler, measure how far west you are from this border. Then use the calculator and the scale of the map to work out how many kilometres (or miles) this is.

You should find:

As you know (it's on page 67), the sun seems to move across the sky at a regular speed. So all you do is divide the distance in kilometres by 20.1 (or miles by 12.5) and you have the number of minutes your local time is behind the official clock time. These are the number of minutes you're allowed to be late. Worth a try – isn't it?

Er – hold on, looks like Norbert's back – what's up?

The sun moves at 335.28 metres (1,100 ft) per second if you want to be astoundingly accurate!

I'm at the west end of this soccer pitch. My local time is now 0.22 seconds behind the east end! Hmm — fascinating!

SIT DOWN! YOU'RE SPOILING THE GAME!

An important announcement for teachers from the publishers

We apologize for the disruption caused by younger readers of this book who are turning up late for classes and claiming that the class clock is wrong. The author responsible is now in hiding.

An important announcement for anyone who thinks that it's possible to get away with being late for things

We have just heard that teachers have worked out that if the local time is later than the clock time then that means that classes can go on later than the clock says...

STOP PRESS ~ We have just heard that children are now claiming that clock time is perfectly OK when it comes to going home from school...

Well, I think it's safe for me to creep out of hiding. I just wanted to say that nowadays we can measure time (time zones and local time) pretty accurately. And we've got some really whizzy watches to help us. I mean, even that oh-so-ordinary-looking watch on your wrist is a little marvel.

Watch this!

A quartz watch works by running electricity from a battery through a tiny piece of manufactured quartz. (Quartz is a type of rock.)

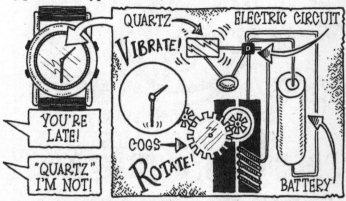

The quartz wobbles (vibrates) 4.25 million times a second at a regular rate. In this way it keeps time and produces pulses of electricity to control the motor that turns the watch hands.

Bet you never knew!
The quartz inside your watch makes a high-pitched whine as it vibrates. This would drive you crazy if your ears were sensitive enough to hear it.

We'll be taking a short break now but don't stop reading – we'll be back in a tick-tock!

Never mind, you can put it on your Christmas list...

At this moment I can guess what you're thinking: you're thinking that time is sorted. Time is tamed and measured and made sense of. After all, we've got watches and time zones and everyone's sure what time it is!

Er, no…

NO?

Yes, you know that bit about a day lasting 24 hours? Well – it's *not quite true*…

Bet you never knew!

The Earth's spin is slowing because of the dragging effect of the sea's tides! This makes each day 0.00000002 seconds LONGER than the day before! Does this explain why Friday afternoons drag on for so long? Anyway, it means even if the world had *managed to celebrate the Millennium in the right year we'd have still fired those fireworks and popped those party poppers at the wrong time!*

TUT, TUT! YOU'VE MISCALCULATED THE CORRECT DAY FOR YOUR CELEBRATION, YOUNG MAN — GO HOME!

Fortunately, the world now has a marvellous bit of science kit to help us keep track of those awkward little milliseconds and keep time so exactly that there are absolutely NO arguments. In fact it's only one second wrong in THOUSANDS of years!

It's called an atomic clock.

Awesome atomic clocks

Here's how an atomic clock works…

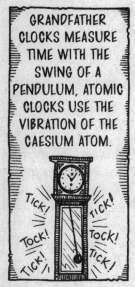

GRANDFATHER CLOCKS MEASURE TIME WITH THE SWING OF A PENDULUM, ATOMIC CLOCKS USE THE VIBRATION OF THE CAESIUM ATOM.

TICK! TICK! TOCK! TOCK! TICK! TICK!

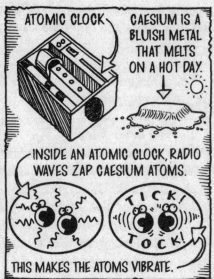

ATOMIC CLOCK

CAESIUM IS A BLUISH METAL THAT MELTS ON A HOT DAY.

INSIDE AN ATOMIC CLOCK, RADIO WAVES ZAP CAESIUM ATOMS.

TICK! TOCK!

THIS MAKES THE ATOMS VIBRATE.

The atomic clock was invented by US scientists in 1948, and clocks were built in the USA and Britain. They were a great success and in 1967 the nations of the world agreed to base time on the wobbling caesium atom.

Today, one second is officially reckoned to be 9,192,631,770 vibrations of caesium and one hour is now about 330,934,743,700,000 (around 33 TRILLION) caesium wobbles. (It might seem longer if you happen to be waiting for a train in the rain.) Time is now clocked by a worldwide system of 50 atomic clocks coordinated by an International Bureau in Paris. And it's as accurate as measuring the distance to the moon to the width of a human hair. Impressive – huh?

This is far more accurate than the Earth's wobbly, ever-changing movements in space. So to keep the official time in line with the Earth, an extra or "leap" second can be added. Yes, Norbert?

Yes, indeed! Every few years, one day is reckoned to have 86,401 seconds instead of 86,400. A whole second... free! Let's celebrate!

So nowadays we're not really measuring time in terms of the Earth spinning in space. It's more to do with a fidgety atom that can't keep still. But you might be wondering why anyone, apart from Norbert, wants to measure time to the nearest billionth of a second. Well, scientists do. Science is about accuracy of measurement and that includes time. And as you'll find out on page 105, time experiments need to be clocked really, *really* accurately.

Navigation systems on planes also need accurate time-keeping. Being one billionth of a second out may mean that you're 30 cm (1 ft) off course. And then you might land in a swamp full of hungry alligators instead of on the runway.

HOLD TIGHT — IT'S CRUNCH TIME!

So the next time you fly you'd better hope that the caesium atoms are wobbling to time.

So that's it…

Thanks to those tireless ticking atoms we can measure time *exactly*. And like a stream, time always flows past at the same speed and we can all set our watches without worrying that time will ever run slower. *No way!* Or as Norbert might say…

You see, the dramatic discoveries of a certain scientific superstar, whom we've already met, have chucked everything back into the melting pot. In fact, time really CAN slow down. It *all depends on how fast you're moving…*

And if that sounds massively mind-stretching you'd best switch your grey cells to overdrive for the next chapter…

Yippee, it's fasten your seat belt time!

TERRIBLY SPEEDY ~~TIME~~

As I was just saying, the rate at which time passes depends on your speed. And the inventor of this incredible idea? Albert Einstein, of course!

To understand what Einstein was on about we'll need to get to grips with his Special Theory of Relativity. And if you thought I just said "the special theory of relatives and tea" you really do need to read on. Albert dreamt up the theory in 1905, the same year in which he proved the existence of atoms.

But wait! I've just heard that our pal MI Gutzache is experiencing the effects of Einstein's Theory! We'll find out what's happening to him in a second, but first there's a word I've just got to explain...

Terrible expressions

A scientist says:

I'M GOING TO MEASURE THIS MASS...

Do you say...?

ISN'T THAT A KIND OF DONKEY?

STAGGER!

WOBBLE!

Answer: NO! That's an ass – you ass! Mass means the amount of material that makes something up. Just remember that something that has a lot of mass tends to be pretty MASS-ive in size...

99

As you're about to find out, mass is a vital idea when it comes to understanding time and space…

M.I. GUTZACHE IS LOST IN TIME (and space)

The story so far…

Fearless private eye MI Gutzache is recovering from a time-travel experiment that went wrong. That night he woke up suddenly…

I knew the Prof had company – and the company wasn't invited. The Prof was snoring but I figured I could handle the situation. I crept into the lab. The Prof's dumb cat followed. But we weren't alone. A little green guy with tentacles was snooping around the machine! Then he blasted the machine with his ray gun.

I knew he wasn't your average two-bit hoodlum, but I decided to play it cool. "Hey, lil' fella," I hissed, "ain't you on the wrong planet?"

Well, I figured ET didn't like my tone. Before I could do nothing he knocked me out with a blast from his ray gun. And next thing I knew I was aboard his flying saucer. Well, I guess that was bad – but the little schmuck kidnapped the cat, too!

When I came to we were in space. The sky was big and black and the stars were kinda shiny. I'd never seen so many stars and the Earth looked mighty small.

Meantime that low-life cat was licking her butt and scratching her fleas. The little green guy said he was Oddblob from the planet Blurb and his orders were to trash the time machine because we humans are too dumb to use the technology wisely.

Well, I kinda took exception…

"Now listen up, wise guy!" I snapped. "This dumb animal here is what you might call stupid. But I'm as smart as the next alien!"

Well, that kinda got Oddblob thinking and he said that in that case I might figure out some simple rules of time and space discovered by a guy named Einstein…

"How fast is the light from our laser headlight?" asked the little fella.

I reasoned for a while and figured I'd cracked the case. It turned out I knew nothing.

"Ha ha – trick question!" I replied. "It's the speed of light plus our speed."

The alien gave me a dirty look. "Foolish humanoid!" he sneered. "It's still only the speed of light! Light shines at the same speed no matter how fast you're moving. Albert Einstein should have told you that!"

SCIENCE NOTE
The speed of light is about 300,000 km (186,000 miles) per second. That means that in one second a ray of light could zoom around the Earth more than SEVEN times!

Then I got kinda mad and started hollering.

"Hey, back off, pal! I never knew this Einstein fella!"

Well, Oddblob wasn't having any of it and what happened next made my stomach heave.

"Einstein predicted the results of travelling at 75% of the speed of light," he said nastily and powered up his engine.

The news was bad. For one thing, I have a motion-sickness problem. But there was no way out and I was the fall guy. The flying saucer shot forward – the stars seemed to leap towards us. I knew we were going fast. My stomach knew it too. Why hell, even the cat looked unwell.

"Our craft appears shorter in the direction of travel," announced Oddblob, showing me a picture on his display screen.

"Our mass increases," he added.

All this science sounded kind of heavy.

SCIENCE NOTE – Gutzache's got it right for once! In Earth's gravity we can measure mass in terms of weight.

The alien hadn't finished. He was showing me some kind of alien video of the Prof's clock on Earth. His green face wore a smug look – but my face was green for another reason.

102

"And our ultra-accurate Blurb time-measurer slows down compared to your primitive Earth clocks."

The alien sure knew his stuff! The hands on the Prof's clock were in speeded-up motion. But I had motion problems of my own…

"Do you have a travel-sickness bag?" I gasped, but the alien was still talking science.

"We do not notice because everything is slower. My two brains and your single primitive brain work slower. If you could be heard on Earth your voice would sound s-l-o-w-e-r a-n-d d-e-e-p-e-r."

I put my hand over my mouth and sweated, *slowly*.

"I can't hold it much longer!" I warned.

Oh no! It looks like Norbert isn't too happy about the story…

There is no proof that aliens exist at all – and as for aliens visiting Earth, this is an unlikely suggestion that rightly belongs in a work of science-fiction!

OK, Norbert, scientists don't believe aliens have visited Earth but most reckon that our galaxy has so many stars that there must be life somewhere. And I should add that the way that time slows down when you travel fast – that is TRUE and scientists have *proved* it happens … honest!

Could you be an Einstein? – part 1*

* *(Part 2 of this quiz is on page 118)*

Can you predict the result of the following experiments…?

1 Muons are tiny bits of matter that exist for two millionths of a second. What do you think happened when scientists made them in the lab?

a) The faster they moved the less time they lasted.

b) The faster they moved the longer they lasted.

c) The slower they moved the longer they lasted.

2 In 1971, two US scientists took atomic clocks on round-the-world trips on planes. What did they find?

a) They landed half an hour before they set off.

b) Time actually slowed down a bit whilst they were in the air.

c) Time speeded up whilst they were flying.

"BIG DEAL!" I hear you exclaim and I'm not too surprised. It's not very much is it? A plane can only fly at one-millionth the speed of light – so if you spent your whole life whizzing about in planes you'd only live one millisecond longer than if you'd stayed on the ground.

But cheer up, you can time travel into the future without leaving the ground … in fact you're forced to!

How you and me and your pet cat are already time travellers

Thanks to the time dilation effect, you and me, your cat and your pet goldfish, and everyone on planet Earth is a time traveller! It's true – at this exact second the Earth is whizzing through space as it loops around the sun, while the sun and the Earth are zooming round the galaxy and the galaxy is sailing around in our local friendly group of galaxies. Feeling dizzy yet?

In all we're moving at 350 km (217.5 miles) per second. That's also a tiny fraction of the speed of light – but it's enough to make each second on Earth last one-millionth longer than it should. And that means if you came from a very sluggishly slow boring planet and spent your life on Earth, when you went home you'd travel 40 minutes into the future!

Time for a quick re-cap. We've looked at how going fast can make time slow down. But Einstein's Special Theory of Relativity went on to change the whole way in which scientists look at time. And we'll be changing our view too, in the next chapter.

SPACED-OUT SPACE-TIME

Do you remember how I said that time is a bit like an onion and this book would peel away the layers and explain what time is really about?

YEAH!

Well, we've just about reached the centre of the vegetable (but don't fry it yet). And this book is about to turn mind-squelchingly head-explodingly brain-boggling … (YOU HAVE BEEN WARNED!)

Brain-boggling space-time

You've heard of space? You've heard of time? Well, in this chapter we're not going to be talking about space and time because in fact time and space go together like toes and ankles. Yep, folks, they're part of the same thing! Scientists call it "space-time" and if your head just turned full circle on your neck, you'd do well to spend some time in the space of the next few pages…

How to get your head round space-time in three (fairly) easy lessons

1 You may know that our world has three directions (or dimensions). There's up-and-down, side-to-side, and front-to-back…

Over the page our ever-helpful artist has drawn a three-dimensional dog to explain what I mean… Thanks, Tony!

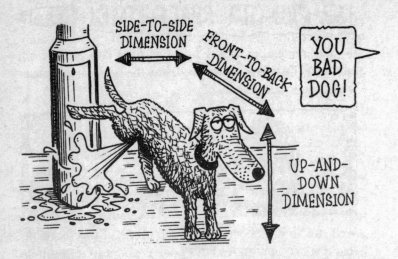

2 In space-time you have to imagine time as the fourth dimension (or direction) in space. Scientists draw a special diagram to show you where you are in space-time:

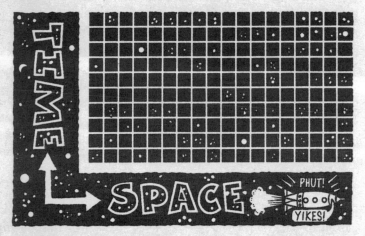

3 Now, the whole point of space-time is that if you're planning a trip in space you really need to know your position in space *and* the time. And here to show you how space-time works are the adventures of Captain Smirk on the star-ship *Terrible*.

CAPTAIN'S LOG

STARDATE: 2090 – 201 days

We're still working on the engine.

A QUICK NOTE FROM THE AUTHOR
Notice anything, readers? The spacecraft has moved on in time by one day but it hasn't moved in space because it's still broken down!

CAPTAIN'S LOG

STARDATE: 2090 – 202 days

The engine is fixed and we have travelled one hundred million kilometres to the planet Thwack!

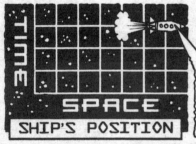

SHIP'S POSITION

WELL DONE – I HOPE THEY SELL TOILET PAPER ON THWACK!!!!

ANOTHER QUICK NOTE ~ The spacecraft has moved on in time another day and moved a MASSIVE distance in space!

You might be wondering where I got this idea of space-time. Did I discover it myself? Oh yeah – I wish. In fact, the idea of space-time came from Albert Einstein's old maths teacher! And he's on the TV show where the guests are late, long-gone and even a bit gone off...

Dead brainy: Hermann Minkowski (1864–1909)

We're linking up live with... Albert Einstein's dead-brainy college maths teacher!

GROAN!

R.I.P.

LIVE BROADCAST

111

IMPORTANT AND URGENT NOTE TO YOUNGER READERS

Don't get any ideas. Missing your maths class and copying your friend's work doesn't make you a genius!

So how did you discover space-time?

AFTER READING EINSTEIN'S SPECIAL THEORY OF RELATIVITY, I REALIZED THAT THE BEST WAY TO EXPLAIN HOW TIME SLOWED DOWN WHEN YOU WENT FAST WAS THAT TIME AND SPACE ARE PART OF THE SAME THING.

And do you remember what you said in 1908?

I SAID, "HENCEFORTH SPACE BY ITSELF AND TIME BY ITSELF, ARE DOOMED TO FADE AWAY INTO MERE SHADOWS, AND ONLY A KIND OF UNION OF THE TWO WILL PRESERVE AN INDEPENDENT REALITY."

WOW! And have you got a message for your most famous pupil?

WHERE'S YOUR MATHS HOMEWORK, YOU LAZY DOG?!

It took time for word about Einstein's Special Theory of Relativity to filter through and meanwhile the man himself was still a clerk. In 1907 he was turned down for a teaching job that wasn't even paid! The following year he got a job teaching science but just three students turned up to his classes! By now, though, he was working on some terribly tricky maths of his own...

The Special Theory of Relativity was all about what happens if you go fast, but it didn't say anything about gravity. So now Albert was looking for a theory that combined the idea of space-time with gravity. It was even harder than it sounds...

For one thing, the maths proved tougher than Albert had bargained for … sounds familiar? Maybe he should have showed up for those maths classes after all! After a few years of struggling with the fiendish figures he admitted:

In desperation, he wrote to his friend, Marcel Grossmann, for help – yes, that's the same friend who had let Albert copy his maths notes:

With the help of Marcel's maths, Albert came to realize that gravity happens because space-time is actually being *pulled towards* an object. Eureka! Albert had hit on his greatest scientific discovery – the Theory of Relativity…

Einstein's terrible joke
Unlike some scientists, Albert had a sense of humour. In 1949 he said: "When you sit on a red-hot cinder a second seems an hour. That's relativity."

Readers keen on time travel are advised not to try this experiment – it has *nothing* to do with relativity. Unlike the facts you're about to read…

Terrible time fact file

NAME: Einstein's Theory of Relativity

THE BASIC FACTS: 1 By 1915, Einstein had proved that any object with mass pulls space-time towards it in the same way that a cat sleeping on your bed makes a dip in the covers.

SPOT THE DIFFERENCE

PULL! & Purrrr!

SPACE-TIME   BED-TIME

2 Whilst it's true that you and your cat pull space-time a teeny bit, if you want *real* pulling power it helps to have massively more mass. Take the Earth, for example.

3 Any passing spacecraft must be drawn towards Earth by the curve of space-time. This is the effect we call "gravity".

HOLD TIGHT EVERYBODY — WE'RE BEING PULLED TOWARDS THAT GREEN AND BLUE BALL!

GRAVITY

THAT'S EARTH, CAPTAIN!

The closer you get to the Earth the more strongly space-time is pulled towards it and that's why you can't escape from Earth by bouncing on a trampoline!

I KEEP TELLING YOU... I NEED A PROPER ROCKET!!!

TERRIBLE DETAILS: When you get something in space with lots of mass squished into a little area then the pull on space-time is so powerful that anyone who goes too close will get their body pulled into bits. (Page 130 has the terrible details.)

YIKES!!!

Dare you discover ... how space-time is curved by mass?

What you need:

A PLASTIC NET BAG FOR VEGETABLES OR THE NET COVERING A SMALL BOX OF FRUIT

A BOWL WITH A RIM THAT CAN BE COVERED BY THE NET

SCISSORS

A LARGE ELASTIC BAND

A TABLE-TENNIS BALL

A RUBBER BALL

What you do:

1 Cut the net open (younger readers may need help here).
2 Place the net over the top of the bowl (this is going to be space-time).
3 Secure it with the rubber band.
4 Place the rubber ball on the net. Remove it and place the table-tennis ball on the net.

You should notice:

The rubber ball has more mass and makes a steeper dip in your space-time. The table-tennis ball forms a larger, more gentle dip. Put both balls on the net and you can imagine they're two planets and create some terrible inter-planetary disasters as they're pulled together! It's all in the cause of science, naturally...

Go-slow gravity

One result of this effect is that an object with lots of mass, like the Earth, actually makes time slow down the closer you get to it. That may sound odd but once again scientists have devised experiments that prove Einstein was *right*...

Could you be an Einstein? – part 2

Which of these experiments actually proves General Relativity and which one is made up and so proves zilch, zippo, nowt and nothing at all?

a) Clocks tested on the moon run faster than clocks on Earth.

b) In 1999, Barry Antley of the University of Duodong delayed the start of the new year on his atomic clock by three milliseconds by living in a hut on top of a mountain for three months.

c) In 1975, Carroll Alley of the University of Maryland took an atomic clock on an exciting all-expenses-paid flight 9 km (5.6 miles) in the air. He found that at this height time runs a few billionths of an hour faster.

THE EXPERIMENT WORKED... WE'RE OVER THE MOON!!

THIS IS GROUND CONTROL... YOU SHOULDN'T BE THAT HIGH!

Answers: a) and **c)** prove the theory because they show that when gravity is weaker time passes more quickly. **b)** is made up. Gravity is slightly weaker on a mountain top so time actually goes a little faster. This means if you lived your life in the mountains your life would be a fraction of a second shorter than if you lived by the sea.

And here's why gravity makes time slow down. The pull of gravity actually robs light of some of its energy. You can test this idea by running up six flights of stairs. As you battle against gravity you might find yourself losing energy too! Now imagine you're looking down on a massive planet. As light struggles up from the surface, anything taking place down there would seem to be happening more slowly.

The more mass the object has, the slower time goes. In fact if you survived on the sun for a week you'd be a second younger than if you'd stayed at home. Mind you, your survival chances would be less than a choccy bar in a microwave oven.

But there are some things in the universe that have such powerful gravity that they actually STOP time in its tracks! I'm talking about *black holes* in space. Their pulverizing power was predicted by a sick scientist with a disgusting disease...

Hall of fame: Karl Schwarzchild (1873–1916)
Nationality: German

Karl was the eldest of five sons. He was a happy lad (oddly enough considering he had four horrible little brothers). His mum was cheerful and his dad was hard working and the whole family rubbed along just fine.

Unlike the rest of the family, who were keen on art and music, Karl became interested in science and saved up his pocket money to buy a telescope. His best friend was the son of one of his dad's pals, who happened to be an astronomer. Soon Karl became madly keen on astronomy and maths. By the age of 16, he was writing scientific articles.

After studying at the Universities of Strasbourg and Munich, Karl became a Professor and worked on measuring the brightness of stars from photographs. His hobbies were all fairly dangerous – he liked nothing better than ballooning, mountaineering and skiing, but he survived all that. He was one of Germany's top astronomers and everything would have been hunky-dory if it hadn't been for the war.

In 1914, Germany went to war with Russia, France and Britain and the ultra-patriotic Karl joined the army. The fact that he was too old to be a soldier didn't bother him. The army used his talents to work out how best to aim long-distance shells in order to kill the most people, but things really went wrong when Karl was moved to Russia. There, he picked up a sickening skin disease that caused huge blisters and made his skin rot.

To take his mind off his pustules Karl read about Einstein's Theory of Relativity and began to have ideas.

Here's a letter that he might have written to Einstein…

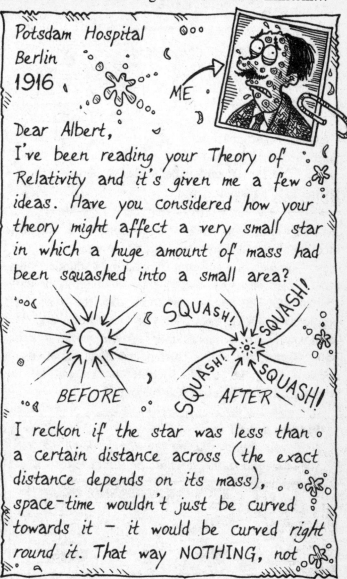

Potsdam Hospital
Berlin
1916

ME

Dear Albert,
I've been reading your Theory of
Relativity and it's given me a few
ideas. Have you considered how your
theory might affect a very small star
in which a huge amount of mass had
been squashed into a small area?

SQUASH!

SQUASH!

SQUASH!

SQUASH!

BEFORE

AFTER

I reckon if the star was less than
a certain distance across (the exact
distance depends on its mass),
space-time wouldn't just be curved
towards it — it would be curved right
round it. That way NOTHING, not

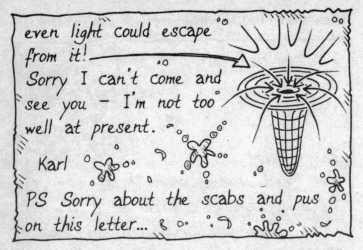

even light could escape from it!

Sorry I can't come and see you — I'm not too well at present.

Karl

PS Sorry about the scabs and pus on this letter...

Einstein read out Karl's suggestion to a scientific meeting, but most scientists didn't agree. Why should they? The idea of a star that trapped light sounded silly.

Karl died of his disease four months later at the early age of 42. But today we know that the stars Karl predicted really do exist. They're black holes and they form when a star collapses under its own gravity to a tiny point. Today, the radius (distance across) of an object needed to make a black hole is known as the "Schwarzchild radius" in Karl's honour.

Bet you never knew!
1 If you could squash the Earth down to its Schwarzchild radius it would be this size...

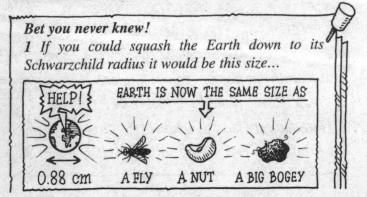

HELP!

EARTH IS NOW THE SAME SIZE AS

0.88 cm   A FLY   A NUT   A BIG BOGEY

At this point the Earth would turn into a black hole! The sun would become a black hole if you squished it into a space 2.9 km (1.75 miles) across. And if you fancy a jumbo-sized black-hole all you have to do is squeeze 500 sun-sized stars into our solar system.

2 Prepare yourself for a shock and try not to let this spoil your day. Scientists reckon there's a HUGE BLACK HOLE in the centre of our galaxy! The black hole is 11.25 billion km (7 billion miles) across! But before you look for a fast rocket out of here I'd better add that it's a big fat well-behaved black hole that's eaten every star near it and is now dozing peacefully like a big contented cat snoozing after supper. Anyway, we won't be going anywhere near it for billions of years.

But here's the interesting thing. If we could go near the black hole we could find the secret of travelling into the future. And with that scary suggestion it's time to tread carefully into the next chapter. By the way, it's all about time travel and I've got a terrible feeling that MI Gutzache and Tiddles might be heading for a black hole! Are they on a one-way trip?

Time travel is not a new idea...

London, 1895

My dear friends,

Everything I told you is true! I am a time traveller and I really did visit the far future. And that story I told you about how we humans end up as two races - a tribe of beautiful but weak beings and a mob of hairy flesh-eating monsters - is true!

PLEASE BELIEVE ME - I AM NOT MAD! Those monsters wanted to EAT ME!

So you wanted to know how I escaped? Well, I shut myself in the monsters' temple and started up my machine. But I panicked, didn't I? In the dark, I set the wrong date on my machine and went far into the future to the time when the sun has died and all life on our planet has ended. Once again I escaped with my life - but only just!

And you, my dear friends, told me to rest and recover but I wanted to

visit the past. So now I'm sitting in my little brass machine and setting the dials to whiz backwards in time. I know it's dangerous but I've just got to do it! And, my friends, if you read this letter it must mean that I never came back. Let this be my goodbye...
So long!

The Time Traveller

And the time traveller was never seen again and perhaps he ended up as a dinosaur's dinner. But don't worry – it's only a story! Mind you, ever since writer HG Wells penned the tale in 1895, people have dreamt of travelling through time. In a moment, we'll find out if time machines really are possible but first you may be shocked to find out that there is a way to see the past happening in front of your eyes! And there's no risk of being a tyrannosaur's tea-time treat either. It's easy when you know how!

All you do is wrap up warm and go outside somewhere dark on a starry night (younger readers should take an adult with them and make sure the adult doesn't get lost or scared). And just gaze at the stars. Aren't they lovely? Who needs boring street lights when we have the stars for free?

OUCH! I DO!

CLONK!

Because the universe is so big, the light from many stars has taken hundreds or thousands of years to reach us. Even our next-door-neighbour star, Proxima Centauri, is about 40,000 billion km (25,000 billion miles) away. And that's so far its light takes 4.25 years to reach us. So when you look at the stars, you don't see them as they are now – you see them as they were in the past when the light left the star. Get the idea?

And yes, that means if you had a really big telescope (bigger than anything that's ever been invented) you might spot weird-looking aliens, wearing embarrassing alien fashions, sporting dreadful alien haircuts, dancing to awful alien disco music 30 years ago. And aliens with their really big telescopes might gaze in horror at your dad's disco dancing 30 years ago!

Yep, you've got it – you and the aliens would both be looking backwards in time!

But of course, looking at an out-of-date view of the stars (and the out-of-date stars on alien TV) isn't half as much fun as real "I was there" time travel. And didn't I mention that a black hole might come in handy here? And didn't I warn you that MI Gutzache and Tiddles would get uncomfortably close to one??

M.I. GUTZACHE IS LOST IN TIME

The story so far…

   MI Gutzache and Tiddles have been abducted by an arrogant alien with two ultra-brainy tentacle brains. Gutzache has been taken unwell…

I felt better after I'd chucked my guts – but the little green guy didn't take it too well.

I had to clean out the craft with some kind of super-sucker alien sponge and just when I'd finished, that dumb useless feline started barfing too. Out of sympathy, I figured.

Well, I guess that made the alien kinda mean 'cos shortly after he tried to rub us out.

He was peering at his control panel and his tentacles started to twitch. I knew he was up to no good. He pulled his ray gun and stuck it under my nose.

"Our sensors show a black hole ahead," he said. "No humanoid has ever entered a black hole. YOU and your fellow earth creature will be the first to try this experiment. Get into the escape craft…"

Then the alien displayed some kind of simulation to show us what to expect. I watched it all and wished I hadn't…

129

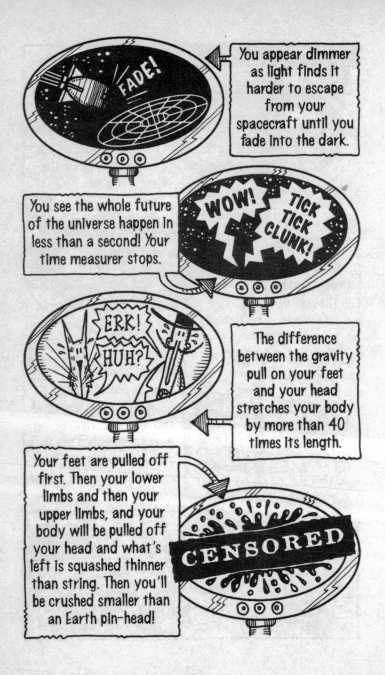

The alien sure wasn't kidding. I figured we were spaghetti – and pasta wasn't my thing. The black hole was no holiday trip. There was no way me or that mangy low-life feline were gonna try it. We both wanted out and that meant staying put.

I was just cooking up a sob story about my aged mom in New York when Dame Fortune dealt a helping hand.

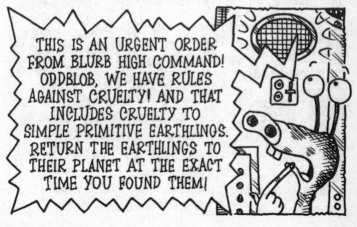

The timing was good. Oddblob didn't like it – but these were orders and the heat was off.

"You'd better take us home, pal!" I told him.

The alien looked glum.

"Our fast space-flight slowed time. Earth is now ten Earth-days in front of us!" he said.

I was just trying to get my head round this when the little green guy brightened up. "I have decided to travel back in time by travelling faster than light," he announced.

Then he bustled about the controls making happy sounds. I guess he liked speeding. Well, we just had time to fasten our safety belts when my stomach shot forward and the stars and space blended into a whirl like froth on a coffee. I grabbed the cat and the cat grabbed me and Jeez her claws were sharper than mine!

I gritted my teeth in pain and looked for the traffic cops. I felt sick but I'd already shot my supper.

"Have you a licence for this thing?" I asked the little guy, but I guess he missed my drift.

And then I figured that if we were going back in time we could hit any year I fancied. Time to cut a deal.

"Hey, buddy!" I said. "Take me back a few years, I could solve the pizza parlour murder mystery! I could win the lottery!"

But the alien wasn't playing ball...

"FORGET IT, EARTHLING!" he replied.

Just then a comet crashed into a mighty big space rock – except we saw it backwards! The comet kinda leapt from the rock.

It put itself together and flew off as good as new! Even that dumb-schmuck cat looked surprised.

In less time than it takes to tell, Oddblob guided the flying saucer back to Earth, arriving at the Professor's house on the night we left. The Prof didn't spot the alien but he sure was mad at the busted time machine. I knew I was in the frame and I sure took the rap...

Uh-ho – Norbert's not too happy about the story and he's wagging his finger.

Oh dear, naughty, naughty! I must point out in the strongest possible terms that NOTHING can go faster than light and no one can go backwards in time!

Oh, er, sorry, Norbert! He's got a point, readers. Remember when Oddblob's spacecraft went fast the first time (it's on page 102)? The craft's mass increased. Einstein's calculations for the Special Theory of Relativity show that mass and energy change into each other at high energies. As the huge energy of going fast turns into mass it becomes harder to go faster. If you really could go as fast as light you'd have more mass than the entire universe!

This would mean two things…

1 You have a serious weight problem and would need to go on a cosmic crash diet.

2 You actually need *endless* energy to go this fast and there isn't that much energy in the whole universe.

So, many scientists think you can't travel faster than light.

I hope you've been making notes on all this…

But – and OK I'll come clean, it's a BIG "but" – some scientists reckon that there may be ways of sneaking around the cosmic light-speed limit. And just imagine if you could! As you know, the faster you go, the slower time passes compared to Earth. So if you could go *faster* than light, it's possible that your clock would actually run *backwards* compared to Earth time! And that actually means you'd be returning in the past – just like in the story!

This idea is explained in a traditional limerick recited by frisky freaky physicists at scientific parties:

There was a young lady named Bright
Whose speed was far faster than light
She set out one day in a relative way
And returned the previous night!

But is it really, honestly possible to travel through time?

Well, it's best to take the question in two parts. If you're talking about travelling *forward* in time, as you've found out, the answer is "yes". We're moving forward into the future anyway and to do some serious forward time travel all we need to do is solve the problem of going *really* fast through space. And we can always slow time by going near (but not too near!) our local friendly snoozing black hole.

ZZZZZZZZ

SSSSH! DON'T WAKE IT!

As for travelling backwards in time, scientists are divided (most would say "NO"). The scientists who would say "YES" or "MAYBE" have their own rather complicated favourite ideas. We'll be back after the commercial break…

What's that? You didn't understand some of the words in these adverts? Well, you'd best read this…

Terrible expressions
A scientist says:

How to build your own time machine

1 First, make a wormhole by creating a black hole and whizzing it around.

2 Take one end of the wormhole for a fast space-flight. You can pull it along by tempting it with a nice juicy planet – Jupiter will do.

3 Thanks to time dilation, when you return to Earth 50 years will have passed, but you can get back to the year when you set off by jumping into the wormhole and leaping out the other end!

It may sound loopy but you've made a loop in time. Don't be scared – it's safe! If you don't touch the sides of the tunnel you won't suffer the black-hole effect!

HI, MUM... GUESS WHAT? I'M GOING TO HAVE FOUR CHILDREN... THREE GIRLS AND A BOY!

The bad news

It's NOT that easy, as Norbert is desperate to point out. OK, Norbert you can put your hand down now.

Tut, tut — this is nonsense! You see, there's not enough energy on Earth to make a wormhole! Anyway how would you stop one closing up? Oh dear, I'm getting quite hot under the collar about this!

Scientists are discussing these problems at this very minute and a few horribly complicated ideas for holding open the wormhole have been suggested. Trouble is, they use types of energy that may not even exist – so don't pack for that last-minute bargain time-travel holiday just yet!

Mind you, one day it might be as easy to time travel as hopping on a bus. In fact, it might be easier because there may not be any buses by then! But would we want to travel backwards in time? If you did manage to go back to *before* you were born, things do get rather *impossible*…

Impossible things that could happen to time travellers

1 A half-crazed time traveller might kill their granny…

PROBLEM: But if she killed her granny, then the time traveller couldn't have been born! By the way, why is it that time science books always feature the granny-killing case? Have some scientists got something *against* grannies?

2 The time traveller might meet her younger self…

PROBLEM: So who is the *real* person?

3 And she might tell herself how to make the time machine.

PROBLEM: So where did the idea come from?

Some scientists think there might be ways round these problems. Others think there aren't – but then scientists don't always agree on things. So, what do you think? And if you're not sure, why not have a think about it?

Finished thinking? OK, let's move swiftly on and imagine you could travel *forwards* in time – that's FORWARDS not backwards. How far could you go? Does time go on for ever? Or will time screech to a grinding halt at some future date? Try not to let it keep you awake at night…

As I said on page 8, scientists reckon that time began with the start of the universe – before then there was no space-time and so no time. So that means we're actually looking at how the *universe* might end. In 1922, Russian scientist Aleksandr Friedmann (1888–1925) came up with three possibilities – which one do you fancy?

1 The universe might stop growing and start shrinking, coming together in what scientists call THE BIG CRUNCH! Good news: it's exciting! Bad news: but very messy!

2 The universe gets bigger for ever. Many billions of years in the future the universe will run out of energy as heat is sucked into space from the stars and planets but the universe goes on growing. Good news: we don't get crunched. Bad news: it's boring!

3 The universe will go on getting bigger but not quite so fast – in fact it'll reach the point where it's hardly getting any larger. Bad news: it's even more boring!

No one can be certain what will happen, but at present scientists think that **2** is the most likely outcome. Of course, scientists will continue to argue about which is the right answer. They'll probably argue until the end of time…

I think we'd better leave them to it.

EPILOGUE: THE END OF TIME

Everyone who has ever lived or *will* ever live is affected by time. And some people find the whole idea of time so amazing that they spend years trying to understand or measure it, or just get their heads round it. Think of John Harrison, or Sandford Fleming, or Luigi Lilio...

This book is called *The Terrible Truth About Time*.

Have you been wondering what the Terrible Truth is?

Well, here it is: time is part of everyday life. We think we know what it is, we can keep track of it with clocks, and measure it with incredible accuracy using atomic clocks... We can develop theories about what time is and how it began, we can dream of being able to travel through time. But ultimately *we don't understand time at all!* We're not sure where it came from or where it's going. We can't say how it operates or why it only goes in one direction.

THE TERRIBLE TRUTH IS THAT TIME IS STILL A MYSTERY!

For anyone trying to make sense of time, that really is terrible! And that's why for scientists time remains the ultimate challenge. When Albert Einstein was a very old man he wrote:

We are in the position of a little child entering a huge library whose walls are covered to the ceiling with books in many tongues...
The child does not understand the languages...
He notes a definite plan in the arrangement of the books, a mysterious order which he... only dimly suspects.

Some people get this feeling every time they open a science book (but hopefully not this one!). In case you're wondering, Albert was talking about the ultimate mysteries of the universe. Including, of course, time.

But one thing's for sure. Slowly, scientists are unravelling time's riddle. And the answer is out there. Somewhere in the universe, somewhere in the cold and dark amongst the glittering stars is the key to the mystery. And one day we'll find it … OH YES, IT'S ONLY A MATTER OF TIME!

ONLY A MATTER OF TIME? WELL, YES, THAT'S ONE THEORY. BUT I SUGGEST THAT ESSENTIALLY THE PRIMARY EXPLANATION IS PROVIDED BY THE INFINITE MASS OF...

SHUT UP!

Books are to be returned on or before
the last date below.

The

As he watched
smoke floa
shape with fou
curving thumb
attached to a bo
trying to find son
over. This was it!
he had feared mor

He was alone in
Green Hand!

Tessa Krailing

The Green Hand

Illustrated by Alex de Wolf

For Elizabeth

Scholastic Children's Books,
Commonwealth House, 1–19 New Oxford Street,
London WC1A 1NU, UK
a division of Scholastic Ltd
London ~ New York ~ Toronto ~ Sydney ~ Auckland

Published in the UK by Scholastic Ltd, 1996

Text copyright © Tessa Krailing, 1996
Illustrations copyright © Alex de Wolf, 1996

ISBN 0 590 13598 8

Typeset by Contour Typesetters, Southall, London
Printed by Cox & Wyman Ltd, Reading, Berks.

10 9 8 7 6 5 4 3 2 1

Chapter 1

At breakfast Dom said, "Mum, I can't go to
school today."

Mum sighed. "Oh, Dom. Why not?"

"Aliens are invading our planet. I heard it
on the radio. They said everyone should stay
indoors and watch TV."

She buttered a piece of toast. "Honestly,
Dom, I can't think where you get your crazy

ideas. I know it's hard, starting a new school in the middle of the summer term, but I'm sure you're going to like it. You'll probably like it a lot better than your old one."

Dom didn't think so. He had hated his old school, where he used to go before they moved house, and he didn't expect this new school to be any better. All schools were the same – big, noisy and full of teachers who expected you to be quick and clever and hardworking. He was none of those things, especially quick. It took him hours to write a story and *weeks* to read a book.

His father came into the room.

"Dom says he can't go to school today," Mum told him. "He says aliens are invading our planet and everyone's been warned to stay indoors. He heard it on the radio."

Dad sat down and helped himself to coffee. "I heard it too, but afterwards they said the aliens had got cold feet and cancelled the invasion." He winked at Dom. "So it'll be safe for you to go to school."

Dom ate his cornflakes very, very slowly. "There's something else," he said. "I think I'm sickening for Chinese chickenpox."

"How strange," said Mum. "I can't see any spots."

"You don't get spots with Chinese chickenpox," said Dom. "That's why it's hard to tell when someone's got it. Lots of people have it without realizing, so they go around spreading germs over everybody. It's very catching."

"So how *do* you know when you've got it?" Mum asked. "What are the symptoms?"

"Well," said Dom, thinking hard, "you find it difficult to swallow. That's why I can't eat these cornflakes. And your heart feels sort of heavy, like it's sinking to the bottom of your stomach. Oh, and you can't move your legs." He tried to get up from the table and fell back on the chair, groaning. "I reckon it'll be days before I can walk properly."

"Oh, bad luck!" Dad said sympathetically.

"And the worst of it is there's only one known cure."

"What's that?" asked Dom.

"No television."

Dom stared at his father. "No television?"

Dad shook his head. "You have to stop watching for at least a week."

"A whole *week*? But that's impossible!"

"It's the only way you'll ever get over it. Otherwise . . ." His father looked grave. "I'm afraid there's no hope."

"You're making it up," Dom said accusingly. "I don't believe you."

"And *I* don't believe either of you!" said Mum. "Now hurry up and finish your breakfast, or you'll be late."

It was no use. He couldn't get out of it. Miserably he got down from the table, collected his peanut-butter sandwiches for lunchtime, and followed his mother out to the car.

He didn't like the look of his new school at all. Part of it was very old – a tall grey building with narrow windows; and part of it was fairly modern. He hoped he would be in the modern part. The old building looked pretty gloomy.

As soon as he got out of the car he could hear the other children shouting and screaming in the playground. "My legs have gone funny again," he told his mother. "I reckon it's that Chinese chickenpox. Please take me home. I don't mind about not watching television."

"Oh, Dom," she said. "It won't be nearly as bad as you think, honestly it won't. Look, here comes your new teacher. Her name's Mrs Lawson and she's very nice. I met her the other day."

Mrs Lawson was short and smiling and brisk. "Hello, Dominic," she said. "Welcome to Grove Road School. Come inside and meet the other children."

Reluctantly he said goodbye to his mother and followed Mrs Lawson into the playground. She called out, "Ian! Ian, come over here."

A boy with a freckled, friendly face came towards them. Mrs Lawson said, "Ian, this is Dominic. I'd like you to look after him, please. Show him where to put his things and then take him into the classroom. He can have that spare place at your table." She

hurried off into the old part of the building.

Ian looked at Dom. "What did she say your name was?"

"Dominic. But people usually call me Dom." He cleared his throat nervously. "What's it like at this school?"

Ian shrugged. "Okay."

"What are the teachers like?"

He shrugged again. "Some are okay, some aren't. Mrs Lawson is mostly okay, although she can be a bit bossy at times. Come on, I'll show you our classroom."

Just as Dom had feared, Mrs Lawson's classroom was in the old part of the school. It was a large room with high, narrow windows. All you could see through the glass were small patches of grey sky.

"You can sit there," Ian said, pointing to a chair.

Dom sat. He was going to hate this school, he could feel it in his bones. It didn't matter how okay Mrs Lawson was, he was going to HATE it!

He cleared his throat and said, "It's a bit spooky in here."

Ian grinned. "This classroom's supposed to be haunted."

Dom stared at him. "Haunted? You mean . . . there's a ghost?"

"Well, part of a ghost. Actually it's just a green hand." Ian sat in the chair opposite and put his feet up on the table. "'Course, I don't believe in it myself, but some people do."

Dom swallowed hard. "Did you say – a *green hand?*"

Ian nodded. "Jenny Jakes swears she saw it only last week. She had to stay in during break because she was behind with her work, so she was in the classroom by herself. Then all of a sudden she came running into the playground, yelling that the ghost had appeared and started writing a message on the board. Mrs Lawson told her not to be silly but Jenny said she definitely saw it."

"Did – did she say what it looked like?"

"Horrible. All green and bony with long knobbly fingers."

Dom swallowed again. "What – what did it write on the board?"

"MRS LAWSON HAS A LONG NOSE." Ian grinned. "'Course, Jenny was mad at Mrs Lawson because she had to stay in during break, so it was pretty obvious she'd written it herself and tried to make out it was the ghost. Least, that's what *I* think."

"Did Mrs Lawson see the message?"

"Yes – and she was *furious*! She said it was a pity Jenny couldn't write as well in her English book as she did on the board." He laughed. "The joke was that she hasn't really got a long nose, but after she'd read the message she kept squinting down it to make sure."

At that moment the bell rang. Ian hastily took his feet off the table just as the other children came racing in from the playground.

"Quiet, everyone!" called out Mrs Lawson when she entered the room. "Take your places quickly and settle down. Half-term's over. It's time to get back to work."

Dom sat silent. This was even worse than he had feared. A gloomy old building, a bossy teacher – *and a ghost*!

Chapter 2

At breakfast next morning Dom said, "Mum,
I can't go to school today."

Mum sighed. "Oh, Dom. Why not?"

"My classroom's haunted by a green hand
that writes rude messages on the board."

She buttered a piece of toast. "Honestly,
Dom, I can't think where you get your crazy
ideas. I'm sure you'll like your new school

when you get used to it."

"But it isn't a new school," Dom protested. "It's old and dark and gloomy. I expect that's why it's haunted."

"You've got to give yourself time to settle down. Things are bound to seem strange at first."

Dom sighed. Things were certainly strange all right – and he was never going to get used to it. Never!

His father came into the room.

"Dom says he can't go to school today," Mum told him. "He says it's old and gloomy and his classroom is haunted."

Dad sat down and helped himself to coffee. "Never mind, it won't be like that for long. They're planning to pull it down."

Mum stared at him. "Planning to pull down the school? Are you serious or is this another of your jokes?"

"Quite serious. I only heard about it yesterday. They're going to pull down the old building and build a brand new one in its place." He winked at Dom. "So that should get rid of any ghosts you've got lurking about in your classroom."

But Dom didn't believe him.

On the way into school he met Ian. "Is it true they're going to pull down the old building and build a new one?" he asked.

"Yes, it's true," said Ian. "And a good thing too, if you ask me."

"When are they going to start?"

"I don't know," said Ian. "Let's ask Mrs Lawson."

As soon as Mrs Lawson had finished calling the register, Ian put up his hand. "Please, Mrs Lawson, when are we going to get our new school?"

"They plan to start work in the summer holidays," she said. "But of course it will take them a lot longer than six weeks to put up the new building, so next term we shall be in temporary classrooms in the playground. We'll be rather cramped, I'm afraid. Still, it'll be worth it eventually, when we get our beautiful new school."

Dom worked it out in his head. The summer holidays. . . That meant they would still be in the old building for six more weeks. Six more weeks in a classroom haunted by a *green hand*!

The first lesson that morning was maths, which wasn't too bad. But then Mrs Lawson said they had to write a story. Dom hated writing stories, not because he couldn't think of a good idea – he had PLENTY of ideas – but because it took him ages to write down what he wanted to say. Also, he wasn't very good at spelling, so that every time he came to a difficult word he stopped and looked at it for at least five minutes, wondering if he'd got it right. When the bell rang for the end of the lesson he had written:

I went to the woods.
I met an alein.
He had spiky hair and big ears
He said do you wank to see my
Spaceship. I said yes.
So he

And that was when the bell rang.

Mrs Lawson stopped by his desk. "Is that all you've written, Dominic?"

He nodded and held his breath. She was certain to tell him he must stay in during break and write some more – and then he'd be all alone in the classroom with the ghostly green hand, like Jenny Jakes.

But she only said, "Well, it's an exciting start. Perhaps you can go on with it next time we have story-writing. By the way, you spell 'alien' like this..." She bent down and wrote ALIEN in large clear letters in the margin. "Now, off you go to break."

Relieved, Dom put the book away in his locker and raced into the playground.

"You were lucky," said Ian, who was kicking a football around. "I thought she'd make you stay in."

"So did I," said Dom. "I like Mrs Lawson. She's okay."

Ian grinned. "I expect she's still being nice to you because you're new. You wait till you've been here a bit longer. She can be a bit of a dragon when she's cross."

And when they went back to the classroom after break Dom saw exactly what Ian meant. Mrs Lawson was looking very dragon-like indeed.

"Sit down," she said sternly. "Now, will someone please tell me who wrote this?"

She pointed to the board where a message was written in strange, loopy handwriting.

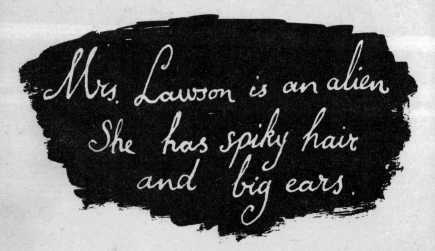

Mrs. Lawson is an alien
She has spiky hair
and big ears.

Everyone stared at the board. Nobody spoke.

Dom went cold all over. Whoever had
written the message must have read his story,
or they wouldn't have known about the spiky
hair and the big ears.

Mrs Lawson said, "And don't tell me it was
the ghost because you know I don't believe in
that nonsense. Was anyone in here alone
during break?"

Very, very slowly one of the girls put up her hand. "Please, Mrs Lawson, I came in to fetch a book. But I didn't write anything on the board."

"Thank you, Fiona. You didn't see anyone else?"

Fiona shook her head. "And I'm sure there wasn't a message on it when I came in because I'd have noticed."

"In that case someone must have come back early from break and written it." Mrs Lawson looked straight at Dom.

He felt himself turning red. It was true he had come into the school building before the end of break, because he had fallen over playing football and wanted to wash the dirt off his hands. But Mrs Lawson obviously thought he had come into the classroom and written the message. He couldn't really blame her. Nobody else had read his story. Nobody else could possibly know that he had written about an alien with spiky hair and big ears.

"Well, I don't intend to make a song and dance about it," Mrs Lawson said with a sigh. "However, if anyone would like to come and own up to me privately I shall be pleased. Dominic, would you please come and clean the board?"

Still red in the face, he did as she asked.

After the lesson Ian asked him, "Did you write that message?"

"No, I didn't!" said Dom.

"But you *did* write a story about an alien. I heard Mrs Lawson tell you how to spell it."

"Well, it wasn't me that wrote on the board. Anyway, it was in funny handwriting, all loopy and curly. I don't write like that."

But he could tell that Ian didn't believe him any more than Mrs Lawson.

So who *did* write the message? The more Dom thought about it the more certain he became.

It must have been written by the green hand!

But why? Why should the ghost deliberately try to get him into trouble by making it look as if it was he who'd said rude things about Mrs Lawson?

He couldn't work it out. It was a complete mystery.

Chapter 3

At breakfast Dom said, "Mum, I can't go to school today."

Mum sighed. "Oh, Dom. Why not?"

"The ghost is trying to get me into trouble. It wrote a rude message on the board about Mrs Lawson and everyone thought it was me."

She buttered a piece of toast. "Honestly,

Dom, I can't think where you get your crazy ideas. I'm sure nobody's trying to get you into trouble. It must have been a mistake."

His father came into the room. "What's this about Dom getting into trouble?" he asked.

"He says somebody wrote something rude on the board and he got the blame for it," Mum told him.

"Well, there's only one answer to that," said Dad. "You have to be bold and fearless, Dom. In other words, you go right up to the person who got you into trouble and warn them that if they do it again you'll report them to the Headteacher."

"I can't," said Dom.

"Why not?"

"It wasn't a person. It was a ghost."

"Makes no difference," said Dad. "Ghosts have to be warned, same as everyone else. You've got to be bold and fearless, Dom. Bold and fearless."

But Dom didn't feel very bold and fearless as he set out for school. To be honest, he felt pretty scared. What if the ghost tried to get him into trouble again? He would have to be very, very careful what he wrote today.

When Mrs Lawson came into class she said, "I've had a brilliant idea."

Everyone sat up and looked at her hopefully.

"Yesterday Ian mentioned our old school being pulled down and it made me think how sad it would be if everyone just forgot about it. So why don't we find out as much as we can, and make a book about its history?"

Everyone looked interested. Well, nearly everyone. Jenny Jakes, who hated any sort of work, yawned and slumped down in her chair.

Mrs Lawson went on, "This building is over a hundred years old, you know. Think of all the children who sat in this classroom when it was new. They were about the same age as you, but they didn't have many of the things you take for granted. No school library, no computers, no heated classrooms in the winter. Some of them had to walk miles to get here. Often they carried two hot potatoes to keep their hands warm – and then they ate them for lunch!"

If he'd had to walk miles to get here, Dom thought, he wouldn't have bothered. He'd have stayed home and watched television. Except, of course, there wasn't any television in those days.

"And when they got to school they had to sit in rows facing the front," Mrs Lawson continued. "Their desks were fixed to the floor and they weren't allowed to move about. They had to sit up straight all the time and keep very, very quiet."

Everyone groaned.

"Oh, yes, it was very different from today," said Mrs Lawson. "Just close your eyes for a moment and try to picture what it was like."

Dom closed his eyes but all he could think
about was the ghost. If the school building
weren't so old it probably wouldn't have a
ghost. The sooner it was pulled down the
better, in his opinion. He couldn't agree with
Mrs Lawson about it being sad.

"Now what I'd like you to do," said Mrs Lawson, "is to imagine yourself back in Victorian times and then write down all the ways it must have been different. Anything you can think of. We'll make that the starting point of our book."

Dom thought hard. After about ten minutes he wrote:

In olden days there was no t.v. The teechers were very

But he couldn't remember how to spell "strict".

When the lesson was nearly over Mrs Lawson stopped by his desk. "Is that all you've written, Dom?" she asked. "Perhaps you'd like to stay in during break and see if you can write a little more?"

Stay in? That was the last thing Dom wanted to do! He was about to say, "No, thanks," when he suddenly remembered what his father had said.

Be bold and fearless, Dom. Bold and fearless.

"Oh, all right," he mumbled.

At least if he stayed in he would be able to wipe off anything rude the ghost wrote on the board before Mrs Lawson had a chance to see it.

But when the other children had gone out to play, and he was left alone in the classroom, he began to feel far from bold and fearless. It was very quiet and the shouts from the playground sounded a long way off. The only noise he could hear was a strange squeaking that seemed to be coming from somewhere nearby. Perhaps it was mice. Well, he wasn't scared of mice, only ghosts.

He bent his head over his book, wishing

he'd asked Mrs Lawson how to spell "strict". Perhaps there was another word he could use. How about "unkind"? Yes, he was pretty sure he knew how to spell "unkind". He finished the sentence:

> In olden days there was
> no t.v. The teechers were
> very unkind.

What *was* that squeaking noise? It sounded like . . . like someone writing with a wet finger on a pane of glass. He looked up and stared round the classroom. No, he was quite alone. But then he noticed a strange smokiness in the air, little curls and whirls of grey smoke billowing around between him and the board, like a mist over marshy ground. Dom watched it, fascinated. Where was it coming from?

As he watched, a shape appeared through the smoke. A floating, wavy, greyish-greenish shape with four long knobbly fingers and a curving thumb. It didn't appear to be attached to a body, but groped around as if trying to find something. Dom went cold all over. This was it! This was the ghostly thing he had feared more than anything.

He was alone in the classroom *with the Green Hand*!

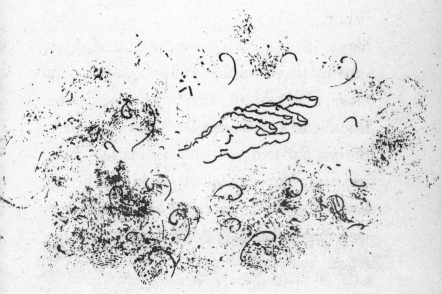

Chapter 4

Impatiently the Green Hand tossed aside a book. It scrabbled among the pens and pencils Mrs Lawson kept in a jar on her desk until at last it found what it was searching for – the chalk. Fascinated, Dom watched as it moved towards the board and wrote:

my teacher is very unkind

"No!" Dom protested. "That's not true. Mrs Lawson isn't unkind. You're just trying to get me into trouble again."

Ha, ha, ha!

wrote the Hand.

Dom remembered something else his father had said. *Ghosts have to be warned, same as everyone else.*

"If you don't wipe that off," he said, "I'll report you to the Headteacher!"

The headteacher has a fat face

wrote the Hand.

Dom was shaking all over. He was sure even his voice was shaking. But he tried to make it sound as fierce as he could.

46

"Wipe it off!" he commanded.

But the ghost only added another word to the sentence. Now it read:

The headteacher has a fat red face

Dom stared at the board in horror. It was true that the Headteacher, who took assembly every morning, had a round, jolly face and sometimes, when he got warm, it did go a bit red. But if Mrs Lawson saw the

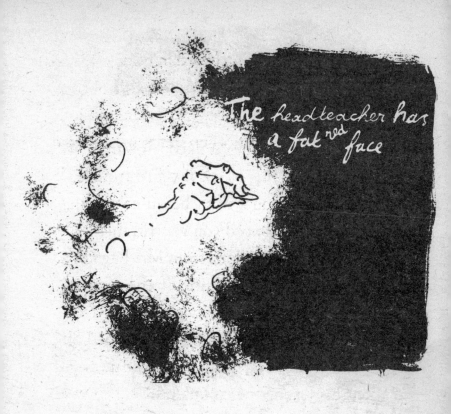

The headteacher has a fat red face

message and thought that Dom had written it. . .

He leapt up from his seat, so angry that he forgot to be scared. "Put down that chalk!" he commanded.

Shan't

the Hand wrote cheekily on the board.

Trembling, Dom walked towards it. "You're just trying to get me into trouble," he said. "Well, you won't – because I'm going to rub out every word you've written!"

He grabbed the cloth from Mrs Lawson's desk and started to clean off the message about the Headteacher having a fat, red face. And when he'd finished that he cleaned off "Shan't!" and "Ha, ha, ha!" and the message about his teacher being unkind.

"There, that'll teach you!" he said, glaring at the Hand. "Now don't you dare write anything rude ever again."

But the Hand only danced away and wrote:

School stinks!

Dom wiped it off.

The headteacher stinks!

wrote the Hand.

Dom wiped it off.

Mrs. Lawson stinks

wrote the Hand, too high for Dom to reach.

At that moment the bell rang for the end of break. Immediately the Hand's knobbly green fingers dropped the chalk on to the desk and the smoke billowed up again into a grey, swirling cloud. When it cleared the Hand had vanished.

Hastily Dom climbed on the chair so that he could reach the last rude message the ghost had written. He was just wiping it off as Mrs Lawson came into the room, followed by the rest of the class.

"Dominic?" she said. "Why are you standing on my chair?"

"Er – I was just cleaning the board," he said.

She looked puzzled. "I don't remember leaving anything on it," she said. "Oh, well, never mind. Go back to your place."

Dom breathed a huge sigh of relief. As soon as he got back to his seat he picked up his pen and hastily changed "teecher" into "teacher". At least the ghost had done him one good turn.

When Ian sat down Dom whispered, "I've just seen the Green Hand."

"Oh, yes?" said Ian, giving him a funny look.

"Actually it's more grey than green. It's pretty spooky, though. And it wrote some really rude messages on the board."

Ian glanced at the empty board. "So where are they?" he asked.

54

"I wiped them off," said Dom. "That's what I was doing when you all came in."

"Huh!" said Ian in a disbelieving sort of a voice.

But Dom felt so proud that he had been bold and fearless enough to stand up to the ghost that he didn't really mind whether Ian believed him or not.

In the afternoon Mrs Lawson said they would go on with their special history project.

"In Victorian times," she began, "the teacher sat at a high desk so that he or she could see everyone. That was important because there were many more children in the class in those days, probably about eighty."

Everyone looked surprised. There were twenty-nine children in Mrs Lawson's class. Dom tried to imagine twice – or even three times – that number in this same room. They must have been squashed in like sardines.

Mrs Lawson went on, "The youngest children learned to write with their fingers in a tray of sand, but when they were old enough they wrote with a special slate pencil on a slate. Can you imagine what a terrible squeaking noise that must have made?"

Dom sat up, remembering the squeaking noise he had heard when he was alone in the classroom this morning. That's exactly what it had sounded like – someone writing on a slate!

"The older children wrote with a pen and ink. But their handwriting had to be very neat and regular, like this. . ." Mrs Lawson turned to write on the board:

This is called copper plate handwriting

Dom stared at it in amazement. What Mrs Lawson had just written on the board looked exactly as if it had been written by the ghost!

"They had to write the same sentence over and over again in a copy book," said Mrs Lawson. "And if they did it badly they were whacked with the cane."

Everyone went, "Oooh!"

"Now, I've had another idea," she went on. "Next Friday we're going to make our classroom as much like a Victorian classroom as we can. We'll arrange the tables so that everyone faces the front and we'll do Victorian lessons. I'll try to get hold of some slates for some of you to write on and the others can use old-fashioned pen and ink."

Ian put up his hand. "Please, Mrs Lawson, are you going to whack us if we make a mistake?"

Mrs Lawson laughed. "No, Ian. We don't have whacking in our school. It's not allowed. But just to make it extra real I'd like you all to come to school in Victorian clothes. I've got a letter for you to take home to your parents, explaining the sort of thing you should wear."

Everyone started to talk at once, but Dom sat silent. He *hated* dressing up.

When the lesson was over he said to Ian, "You know that writing Mrs Lawson did on the board? That's exactly how the Green Hand writes."

"Oh, yes?" said Ian, in his disbelieving voice.

"You realize what this means, don't you?"

"That Mrs Lawson is really the Green Hand?"

"No, stupid! It means that the ghost must be left over from Victorian times. That's why it does that sort of loopy handwriting."

Ian yawned. "'Bye, Dom. See you tomorrow."

On the journey home Dom kept thinking about the Green Hand's strange copperplate handwriting – and that squeaking noise, like someone writing on a slate. He shivered. It was all a bit too spooky for his liking.

As for dressing up in Victorian clothes. . . He fingered the letter in his pocket. Perhaps he needn't even show the letter to his parents. Perhaps he could just forget about it.

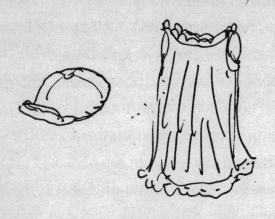

Chapter 5

On the following Friday Dom said, "Mum, I can't go to school today."

Mum sighed. "Oh, Dom. Why not?"

"Everyone's wearing Victorian clothes and I don't have any."

She buttered a piece of toast. "Honestly, Dom, I can't think where you get your crazy ideas. What do you mean, everyone's wearing

Victorian clothes?"

Dom went rather red. "It's for our history project. There was a letter about it."

"Well, *I* haven't had any letter." She gave him a hard look. "Where is it, Dom?"

"In my pocket," he mumbled.

"Show me."

He pulled out the crumpled sheet of paper and handed it to her.

While she was reading it his father came into the room.

"Dom says he can't go to school today," Mum told him. "The others are all wearing Victorian clothes and he forgot to give me this letter about it."

"What sort of Victorian clothes?" asked Dad.

Mum gave him the letter. "It says that girls should wear pinafores and boys should come in ragged trousers and caps."

"That shouldn't be too difficult," said Dad. "I've got a pair of old corduroys we could cut down and I'm sure we can find a cap."

Dom was a few minutes late for school, but it didn't matter. Everyone else was late too, because it had taken them longer than usual to get dressed.

"Oh, splendid!" Mrs Lawson said when she

saw him. "You look just like a real Victorian schoolboy!"

Dom stared round at the rest of the class. Everyone looked quite different from their normal selves, the girls in their pinafores and the boys in their ragged trousers and caps. Even Mrs Lawson looked a completely different person in a long black dress with a high collar.

"Everyone sit up straight," she said sternly. "No one must slouch over their desk today. Remember, you're Victorian children now and Victorian teachers were *very* strict. Have you noticed the portrait that hangs in the hall?"

Everyone nodded. They had all noticed the dark gloomy portrait of a man in a long black gown with a mortarboard on his head. He had bushy eyebrows, a hooked nose and very fierce eyes which seemed to glare at them every time they walked past.

"Well, his name was Mr Quibble," Mrs Lawson told them, "and he was the Head-teacher of Grove Road School a hundred years ago. People say he was the strictest teacher the school has ever had and he used to whack children if they got their sums wrong."

Fiona put up her hand. "I'm glad he's not

Headteacher now," she said. "I'd hate to be taught by Mr Quibble."

Mrs Lawson laughed. "Aren't you *all* glad you're not being taught by Mr Quibble?" she asked the class.

Everyone said, "YES!"

"Now, I've managed to find two slates for you to try. Jenny, would you like to have one of them? Dominic, you can have the other. I'm afraid I couldn't get any slate pencils so you'll have to use chalk."

Dom stared miserably down at the slate she had given him. He knew why she had chosen him and Jenny Jakes. It was because they were the slowest workers in the class and there wasn't much room to write on the small, square slates.

After a while Mrs Lawson stopped by his table. "Oh, Dominic! You haven't written a single word!"

"Can't think of anything," he mumbled.

"In Victorian times they were very fond of sayings like: 'Think before you speak' or 'Children should be seen and not heard'. Why don't you write one of those?"

"All right," he mumbled.

Mrs Lawson moved away, her long skirt rustling as she walked.

Dom found it hard to write on the slate. Twice he tried but he had to wipe it off both

times. The third time he got as far as "Children should be seen" but his writing looked untidy, nothing like the beautiful copperplate handwriting the Victorians used to do. He stopped trying and gazed out of the window instead. It was getting rather misty, he noticed. Misty and smoky. Perhaps someone outside had lit a bonfire?

Mrs Lawson stopped by his desk again. She stared down at the slate. "It's very well written," she said, sounding puzzled. "But don't you think it's rather rude?"

He looked at what he had written. There, in beautiful copperplate handwriting, was the sentence:

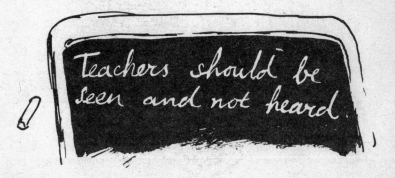

Teachers should be seen and not heard

"I didn't write that!" he said. "I wrote 'Children should be seen and not heard.' But I stopped because I couldn't spell 'heard'."

"You seem able to spell it perfectly now," Mrs Lawson said coldly. "Please wipe it off and write instead, 'Good manners cost nothing.' And I think you'd better stay here until you've done it."

At that moment the bell rang for break. She swept off in her long skirt and the other children ran out of the classroom, leaving Dom alone.

"It wasn't me," he muttered. "I didn't write that, I *know* I didn't. It must have been the ghost."

Suddenly he realized that the grey smokiness he had noticed earlier wasn't outside the window after all. It was inside the classroom, swirling around and getting thicker and thicker. "Oh, no!" he groaned. "Not again!" But this time he felt more angry than frightened. *Be bold and fearless*, he told himself, *bold and fearless*.

"Why do you keep trying to get me into trouble?" he asked loudly. "And why do you haunt this classroom anyway?"

The smoke billowed up and took the shape of the Hand, all greyish-green and knobbly-fingered. It picked up the chalk and wrote on the board:

hate children!

"But *why?*" asked Dom. "Why do you hate children?"

children hate me!

There was quite a loud bang as the Hand added the exclamation point.

Dom stared at it, thinking hard. Then he said slowly, "I know who you are! You're the teacher in the portrait who used to whack people. You're Mr Quibble!"

At his words the smoke billowed up again, swirling around the Hand. Dom shrank back in his seat. Fascinated, he watched as the Hand became attached to a sleeve, and the sleeve to a jacket beneath a long, greeny-black gown. Then, gradually, inside the gown

appeared the misty shape of a man – a tall, thin, stooped man with a hooked nose and a fierce expression.

It was the ghost of Mr Quibble!

Chapter 6

The ghost glared at Dom.

"Yes, I'm Mr Quibble," he said in a hoarse, crackly voice that sounded as if it hadn't been used for about a hundred years. "And kindly call me Sir when you speak to me!"

Dom was too surprised to speak at all. Mr Quibble was wearing exactly the same clothes as in his portrait in the hall – high stiff collar, a long black gown and a mortarboard on his head with a tassel in one corner. The only difference was that he now held in his hand a thin, bendy, nasty-looking cane.

"What are you staring at, boy?" demanded Mr Quibble. "Haven't you been told it's rude to stare?"

"I – I'm sorry," said Dom.

"*Sir!*" snapped Mr Quibble.

"Sir," Dom added hastily. "It's just that I – I've never seen a ghost before. Please may I ask a question?"

"You may ask." Mr Quibble tapped the cane thoughtfully against the palm of his hand. "I may choose not to answer."

"If you hate children why did you become a teacher?"

"I didn't hate them when I started. It was only after years and years of trying to knock some sense into their stupid heads that I grew to dislike them." Mr Quibble glared round the classroom. "So many children, all writing away on their wretched squeaky slates . . . it was like being in a cage full of monkeys."

Dom remembered that Mrs Lawson had told them there were sometimes as many as eighty in a class. He tried to imagine what eighty children writing on slates must have sounded like and shuddered. The very idea of it set his teeth on edge.

"And when they chanted their arithmetic tables it used to give me a terrible headache." Mr Quibble groaned as if he could feel the pain even now. "I'd have given up if I could, but there was nothing else for me to do. I had to go on teaching for the rest of my life."

"But if you hated it so much why do you keep coming back to haunt the place?" Dom asked.

Mr Quibble glared at him. "Stupid boy! If I were your teacher you wouldn't *dare* to ask such an impertinent question."

"But you're not my teacher," Dom said boldly. "Mrs Lawson is – and she's a much better teacher than you ever were."

A look of fury came over Mr Quibble's face. "Come here, boy!"

Reluctantly Dom rose from his seat. Walking towards the ghost was probably about the boldest and most fearless thing he had ever done in his life. His legs felt weak and trembly, as if he had just run a five-mile race.

Close up, Mr Quibble looked very grey and shadowy. He flexed the cane between his green knobbly fingers. "Such rudeness must be punished – and punished severely. Hold out your hand."

Dom shook his head, although his heart was beating fast. "We don't have whacking in our school. It's not allowed."

"Six whacks for rudeness and *ten* for disobedience!" roared Mr Quibble. He raised the cane threateningly above his head. "HOLD OUT YOUR HAND!"

Dom gulped. "You – you can't hurt me. That cane's not real. It's only the ghost of a cane." Nervously he held out his hand, palm upwards. "Go on, try to whack me if you want to. You'll see."

Mr Quibble's eyes blazed with anger. He gripped the cane and brought it down with such speed that it made a whistling sound in the air . . . but when it reached Dom's hand it passed right through. All Dom felt was a little feathery sensation, as if he had been touched by the wings of a moth.

Mr Quibble gave a cry of anguish. He dropped the cane on the floor and collapsed into the teacher's chair, burying his head in his hands.

Dom stared down at him, not knowing quite what to say. After a few moments he cleared his throat and asked the same question as he'd asked before. "If you hated teaching so much why do you keep coming back to haunt this place?"

"I have no choice," Mr Quibble groaned. "That's what happens to the teachers nobody likes. They're forced to keep coming back for as long as the school still stands."

"Well, it won't be standing much longer. They're pulling it down at the end of this term. So then you'll be free to go."

Mr Quibble raised his head from the desk. "While the building stands I still have a chance to break free. Once it's pulled down I'm doomed for ever and ever."

He looked so desperate that Dom felt almost sorry for him. "What do you have to do to break free?" he asked.

Mr Quibble screwed up his face as if what he was about to say really disgusted him. "I have to be kind to someone."

"Anyone?"

"A – a *child*," he said, as if it were the most hateful thing in the world.

"Well, you haven't been very kind to any of us so far," Dom pointed out. "All you've done is try to get us into trouble."

Mr Quibble gave a helpless shrug. "It's all I know how to do."

Dom thought for a moment. Then he remembered what was still written on his slate:

Teachers should be seen and not heard.

He said slowly, "Perhaps, if you changed the word 'teachers' on my slate to 'children', so that I didn't get into trouble again – that might count as being kind to me."

Mr Quibble looked suddenly hopeful. "Do you really think so?"

"Yes, I do. Wait, I'll bring it up to you."

Dom fetched the slate and watched, fascinated, as the ghost's greyish-green hand wiped out the word "teachers" and replaced it with "children".

"Perhaps," Dom added, even more boldly and fearlessly, "you could write something else, so that Mrs Lawson doesn't think I've been wasting time."

"Something *else*?" Mr Quibble glared up at him from under bushy grey eyebrows. "What, for example?"

"I don't know. Another sentence . . . the sort of thing children used to write when you were a teacher." He added quickly, "Please, sir."

After a minute Mr Quibble handed him the slate. Beneath the original sentence he had written:

Children should be
seen and not heard.
A stitch in time
saves nine.

"Will that do?" he asked.

"That'll do fine," said Dom. "Mrs Lawson will be really impressed."

"You like her, this teacher of yours?"

"Oh, yes," said Dom. "She can be strict, but most of the time she's pretty kind."

The ghost heaved a long, wistful sigh. "It must be nice to be liked . . ." But even as he spoke he began to fade, becoming hazier and hazier until finally he disappeared altogether.

"Er – Mr Quibble?" said Dom.

No answer.

"Mr Quibble, have you gone?" asked Dom.

But the only sound he could hear was the bell in the playground sounding the end of break. He glanced down at the floor and saw that the cane had disappeared as well.

By the time the children came rushing into the classroom Dom was back in his seat. "The ghost was here again," he told Ian. "And guess what – it was Mr Quibble! You know, the teacher whose portrait hangs in the hall."

"Oh, yes?" said Ian.

"But this time I saw all of him, not just his green hand. He was very tall and thin, and he wore a long black gown like teachers used to wear in olden times. And he tried to whack me, but the cane went right through my hand!"

"Oh, yes?" said Ian again.

"Actually I felt quite sorry for him. It can't have been much fun, trying to teach eighty kids all at once. That's why he ended up hating them. Anyway, he's gone for good now. He just had to do one kind thing, so I asked him to write on my slate."

"Oh, yes?" said Ian, glancing at Dom's slate. "And I suppose he also wrote that word on the board?"

Dom looked at the board. Just one word was written there:

Goodbye

On Monday morning Dom sat down at the breakfast table and started eating his cornflakes. "I'm really looking forward to school today," he said. "We're going to start making a book about what it was like in Victorian times."

Mum stared at him. "Dom, are you feeling all right?" she asked.

"Yes, why?"

"Oh . . . no reason," she said.

His father came into the room.

"Dom says he's really looking forward to school today," she told him. "They're making a book about what it was like in Victorian times."

Dad sat down and helped himself to coffee. "Pretty awful, from what I've heard. The lessons weren't very interesting and the teachers were much stricter than they are today."

"That's because they had terrible headaches," said Dom. "With eighty children in one room, all writing on squeaky slates and chanting their tables – it was like being in a cage full of monkeys."

Mum looked at him wonderingly. "Honestly, Dom, I don't know where you get your crazy ideas!"

The End